# SACRED SONGS OF INDIA

# SACRED SONGS OF INDIA

V.K. SUBRAMANIAN



ABHINAV PUBLICATIONS

abhinav publications

First Published in India 1996



*Publishers*
Shakti Malik
Abhinav Publications
E-37 Hauz Khas
New Delhi-110016

ISBN 81-7017-321-3

*Phototypeset in Chanakya 12pt and Baskerville 10pt by*

Tara Chand Sons
Naraina, New Delhi

*Printed at*

D.K. Fine Arts Press P. Ltd.
Ashok Vihar, New Delhi

*To my late brother, V.K. Rajagopal*
*whose spirituality, sincerity*
*and spontaneity made him so lovable*

## CONTENTS


| | | |
|---|---|---|
| | Introduction | 9-10 |
| | Acknowledgements | 11 |
| 1. | Songs of Andal (7th century A.D.)—30 Songs | 13-75 |
| 2. | Songs of Jayadeva (12th century A.D.)—10 Songs | 77-123 |
| 3. | Songs of Vidyapati (14th-15th century A.D.) —10 Songs | 125-147 |
| 4. | Songs of Kabir (15th-16th century A.D.)—10 Songs | 149-171 |
| 5. | Songs of Meera (15th-16th century A.D.)—10 Songs | 173-195 |
| 6. | Songs of Purandharadasa (15th-16th century A.D.) —10 Songs | 197-219 |
| 7. | Songs of Surdas (15th-16th century A.D.) —10 Songs | 221-243 |
| 8. | Songs of Tulsidas (16th-17th century A.D.) —10 Songs | 245-267 |
| 9. | Songs of Tukaram (17th century A.D.)—10 Songs | 269-291 |
| 10. | Songs of Tyagaraja (18th-19th century A.D.) —10 Songs | 293-321 |

# INTRODUCTION

The sacred songs of India, included in this book, are an arbitrary, incomplete, whimsical selection, spanning twelve centuries and covering various regions of India.

The only running thread in these songs is devotion to the chosen Deity: Krishna who is also Rama.

The saints who have composed these songs were all mystic poets who dreamed of their beloved deity in uninhibited imagery.

Both Andal—who was born in the South in the seventh century, the daughter of a temple priest—and Meera, the royal princess of Rajasthan who lived in the fifteenth-sixteenth centuries—desired union with Krishna and sang of Him as the Lover.

Jayadeva, the Orissan poet of the 12th century and Vidyapati, the Bihari saint of the 14th century, infused their songs with profuse eroticism about the love of Radha and Krishna—joy in union and sorrow in separation—Radha and Krishna being symbols of the individual soul and the Supreme Spirit.

Purandharadasa, Surdas and Tukaram treated themselves as the servants of the Lord and sang of the glories of their Master.

Kabir's songs are more philosophical in content, though rich in devotion.

Tulsidas and Tyagaraja blindly adored their Rama and sang of His glories with unparalleled intimacy.

The beauty of these songs has transcended the barriers of language, region and time.

Andal sang in *Tamil,* Jayadeva in *Sanskrit,* Purandharadasa in *Kannada,* Tukaram in *Marathi,* Tyagaraja in *Telugu* and the others in various dialects of *Hindi.*

Jayadeva's songs are sung in the temples of Kerala as also in the palace precincts of Rajasthan.

Meera's *bhajans* and Tukaram's *abhangs* are sung by Carnatic musicians of South India in their music concerts.

I consider these songs as great integrating factors and am proud to present them on a common platter to be read, sung and heard, and choreographed and danced by artistes and appreciated by people of all countries, whatever be their religion, race, language or nationality.

Madras

**V.K. Subramanian**

## ACKNOWLEDGEMENTS

This book would not have been possible but for the loving assistance rendered by my friend, Sri R. Swaminathan, in writing out the songs in the Devanagari script and transliterating them into English. I am very grateful to him for this and also prodding me to take up this project and complete it in record time. Working with Sri Swaminathan on this book has been a great joy.

My thanks are also due to Sri Bhajana Bhushana M.O. Srinivasan (a former Test cricketer) for helping me in the selection of songs and setting them in appropriate ragas.

I would like to thank Mrs. Nandini Kapdi I.A.&A.S., for helping me with the translations of Purandharadasa's songs in Kannada.

I am also indebted to Mrs. Snehalata Datar for helping me in translating the songs of Tukaram in Marathi.

I am also grateful to Dr. Rama Shankar Pandey and Abha Goyal for help rendered in the translations of the songs of Kabir, Surdas and Tulsidas.

Madras **V.K. Subramanian**

# SONGS OF ANDAL

*(7th Century A.D.)*

| | *Song* | *Rāga* |
|---|---|---|
| 1. | Margazhi Thingal | Nattai |
| 2. | Vaiyattu | Gowla |
| 3. | Ongi Ulagalanta | Arabi |
| 4. | Aazhi Mazhai | Varali |
| 5. | Mayanai | Sri |
| 6. | Pullum Silambinkan | Sankarabharanam |
| 7. | Keecu Keecendrengum | Bhairavi |
| 8. | Keezhvanam | Dhanyasi |
| 9. | Tumani | Hamir Kalyani |
| 10. | Nottrucchuvargam | Todi |
| 11. | Kattrukkaravai | Huseni |
| 12. | Kanaittilam | Kedaragowla |
| 13. | Pullinvai | Atana |
| 14. | Ungal Puzhakkadai | Ananda Bhairavi |
| 15. | Yelle Ilankiliye | Begada |
| 16. | Nayakanai | Durbar/Mohanam |
| 17. | Ambarame | Kalyani |
| 18. | Undu madakalitran | Saveri |
| 19. | Kuttuvilakkeriya | Sahana |
| 20. | Muppattumuvar | Cenjuriti |
| 21. | Yetrakalangal | Nadanamakriya |
| 22. | Anganma | Yamuna Kalyani |
| 23. | Mari malaimulanchil | Manirangu/Bilahari |
| 24. | Andrivvulagam | Sindhubhairavi |
| 25. | Oruttimakanai | Behag |
| 26. | Male Manivanna | Kuntalavarali |
| 27. | Koodaraivellum | Poorvi Kalyani |
| 28. | Karavaigal | Kamboji |
| 29. | Sitram sirukale | Malayamarutam/Madhyamavati |
| 30. | Vangakkadal | Churuti |

*ANDAL*

## ANDAL (7th century A.D.)

Andal's songs are imbued with bridal mysticism. Her life-history is misty with legends and myths. She was supposed to be discovered as an infant lying under a Tulsi (Basil) plant by the temple priest, Perialwar, also known as Vishnuchitta. Her birth date has been assigned by modern scholars to the middle of 7th century A.D.

The Vishnu temple at Srivilliputtur (some sixty kilometres from the modern city of Madurai) was where Andal developed her bridal devotion. Daily she would deck herself with flower garlands and imagine herself to be the bride of Krishna. In her imagination, she went back to the times when Krishna sported with Gopis in Gokula on the banks of the Yamuna river.

She deemed herself to be a Gopi, rising early in the morning, waking her companions from sleep, having a ritualistic bath and going to Nandagopa's residence to pay homage to Krishna. This imagery is the central theme of *Tiruppāvai,* a string of 30 songs.

Legend has it that Andal was taken in bridal attire to Sri Ranganatha's temple at Srirangam, where she entered the *sanctum sanctorum* and got merged with the Lord.

The temple at Srivilliputtur today houses the images of Ranganatha and Andal, as the Lord and His spouse, where thousands throng to worship, especially during the month of Margasirsa (December 15 to January 15).

Recitation of Andal's 30 songs of *Tiruppāvai* is resorted to by women of South India during this period.

राग : नाटै

Rāga : Nātai

1. मार्गलि़त्तिंगळ् मति निरैन्द नन्नाळाल्
नीराडप्पोदुवीर् पोदुमिनो नेरिलै़यीर्!
शीर्मल्गुं आयप्पाडिच्चेल्वच्चिरुमीर्गाळ!
कूर्वेल् कोडुन्तोलि़लन् नन्दगोपन् कुमरन्
एरान्दं कण्णि यशोदै इळंचिंगम्
कार्मेनिच्चेंकण् कदिर्मदियम् पोल् मुखत्तान्
नारायणने नमक्के परै तरुवान्
पारोर् पुगल़प्पडिन्देलोरेम्पावाय्॥

Mārgazhittingaḷ mati niṛainda nannāḷāl
nīrāḍappóduvīr! pódumino, nérizhaiyīr!
sīrmalgum āyppāḍiccélvaccirumīrgāl!
kūrvél koduntozhilan nanda go pan kumaran
Yérārnda kaṇṇi yaśodai ilancingam
kārméniccéngaṇ kadirmadiyam pol mukhattān
Nārāyaṇané namakké parai taruvān
pāror pugazhappaḍindélorémpāvāi.

1. This is the month of Margasirsa. It is the auspicious full moon day.
Let us go bathing, O! Beautiful girls, adorned with gorgeous ornaments, who are the pride of evergrowing Gokula!
The son Nandagopa (ever vigilant with his sharp spear), the young lion, who is feast to the beautiful eyes of Yasoda,
whose body is cloudhued, the Lotuseyed One,
whose face is like the moon, Sri Narayana, the abode of all beings, will bless this ritual of ours;
the onlookers will praise us. Join us.

राग : गौल Rāga : Gowla

2. वैयत्तु वाऴ्वीर्गाळ ! नामुम् नं पावैक्कु
चेय्युम् किरिशैगळ् केळीरो ! पार्कडलुळ्
पैयत्तुयिन्र परमनटि पाडि
नेय्युण्णों पालुण्णों नाट्कालै नीराडि
मैयिट्टेलुतों मलरिट्टु नां मुडियोम्
शेय्यादन शेय्यों तीक्कुरळै च्चेन्रोदोम्
ऐयमुं पिच्चैयुं आन्दनैयुं कै काट्टि
उय्युमारेण्णि उगन्देलो रेम्पावाय् ॥

Vaiyaṭtu vāzhvīrgāḷ nāmum nam pāvaikku
ccēyyum kiriśaigal kēlīro! pāṛkaḍaluḷ
paiyattuyinṛa paramanaḍi pāḍi
néyyuṇṇom pāluṇṇom nāṭkāl nīrādi
maiyiṭṭézhudom malariṭṭu nām muḍiyom
śeyyādana séyyom tīkkuṛalai cchénrodom
aiyamum picchaiyum āndanaiyum kai kāṭṭi
uyyumāṛeṇṇi ugandélo rémpāvāi.

2. O! All those born to live in this world!
Listen to the disciplines of our ritual!
We shall sing praises of the feet of our Lord
who, is resting on the milky ocean.
We shall not take ghee or milk
We shall bathe early in the morning
We shall not decorate our eyes with collyrium,
We shall not wear flowers on our hair
We shall not do anything which is proscribed,
We'shall not utter words which pain others,
We shall generously give gifts and alms,
Think about all this and be delighted to join us in our ritual.

राग : आरभि

Rāga : Ārabhi

3. ओंगि उलगळन्द उत्तमन् पेर्पाडि
नांगळ नं पावैक्कुच्चाट्रि नीर् आडिनाल्,
तींगिन्रि नाडेल्लां तिंगळ् मुम्मारि पेय्तु
ओंगु पेरुञ्चेन्ने लूडु कयल् उकळ
पूंकुवळै प्पोतिल् पोरिवण्डु कण्पडुप्प,
तेंगाते पुक्किरुन्दु शीन्र्द मुलै पट्रि
वांगक्कुडं निरैक्कुं वळ्ळल् पेरुं पशुक्कळ्
नींगात शेल्वं निरैन्देलोरेंपावाय् ।

Ongi ulagaḷanda uttaman pérpādi
Nāngaḷ nam pāvaikkuccāṭri nīr āḍināl,
Tīnginri nādellām tingaḷ mummāri péydu
Ongu péruncenné lūdu kayal ukaḷa
pūnkuvaḷaippódil poṛivaṇḍu kaṇpaduppa
Téngāté pukkirundu śīrnda mulai patri
Vāngakkudam niraikkum vaḷḷal pérum paśukkaḷ
Nīngāta śelvam niṛaindelorempāvāi.

3. Singing the praises of the Supreme One
who measured the three worlds with his feet
(in His incarnation as Vāmana*),
if we take our ritualistic bath,
the whole country will be free from evil,
there will be three rain showers every month,
In the highgrown paddy fields, fish will leap about,
Bees will sleep within beautiful blooming lotus flowers,
When the milkmen strike at the udders, cows will fill
the pots with milk,
There will be everlasting prosperity.

*INCARNATION AS VĀMANA

King Bali, a descendant of Prahlada, became the master of all the three worlds, defeating the devas (celestial angels). Aditi, mother of the devas, prayed to Vishnu, who promised help and was born as her son, Kasyapa being the father.

Bali was performing the Aswamedha sacrifice, when the young son of Kasyapa and Aditi went and on being asked reverentially by Bali as to what gifts would please him, asked for earth, measurable by three steps of his feet. When Bali made the gift, the dwarfish young boy grew to cosmic dimensions and covered all the worlds with his two steps and proceeded to place his third step on Bali's head, Prahlada appeared and pacified the Lord, who blessed Bali that he would become Indra in another age. This is the story of Vishnu's incarnation as Vāmana, the dwarf.

राग : वरालि

Rāga : Varāli

4. आऴि मऴैक्कण्णा! ओन्रु नी कैकरवेल्
आऴियुळ् पुक्कु मुगन्दु कोडार्त्तेऱि,
ऊऴि मुतल्वन् उरुवंपोल् मेय्करूत्तु
पाऴियन्तोळुडै प्पर्पनाभन् कैयिल्
आऴि पोल् मिन्नि, वलंपुरिपोल् निन्रदिर्न्दु,
ताऴादे शार्ङ्गं उदैत्त शरमऴैपोल्
वाऴ उलगिनिल् पेय्तिडाय्, नांगळुम्
मार्गऴि नीराड मगिऴ्न्देलो रेम्पावाय्॥

Āzhi mazhaikkaṇṇā! onru nī kaikaravél
Āzhiyuḷ pukku mugandu koḍārttéṛi,
Ūzhi mudalvan uruvampol méykaṛuttu
Pāzhiyantoḷudaip parpanābhan kaiyil
Āzhi pol minni, valampuripol ninṛadirndu
Tāzhādé Śārngam udaitta śaramazhai pol
Vāzha ulaginil péydiḍāi, nāngalum
Mārgazhi nīrāda magizhndélo rempāvāi.

4. O! Raingod! Do not forget anything!
Enter the ocean, carry the waters with aplomb,
Ascend the sky, dark as the form of our Lord,
Who is the primal cause of all,
Shine like the discus in the hands of
Padmanabha, who has beautiful shoulders,
Thunder like His conch,
And rain like the shower of arrows from His bow Saranga,
for the sustenance of life on earth,
and to enable us to have our ritualistic bath
during the month of Margasirsa.

राग : श्री

Rāga : Sri

5. मायनै मन्नु वडमदुरै मैन्दनै,
तूय पेरुनीऱ् यमुनैत्तुऱैवनै,
आयर्कुलत्तिनिल् तोन्रुं अणि विळक्कै,
तायैक्कुडल् विळक्कं शेय्त दामोदरनै,
तूयोमाय्वन्तु नां तूमलर्तूवित्तोऴुदु
वायिनाल् पाडि मनत्तिनाल् चिन्दिक्क
पोय पिऴैयुं पुगुत्तरिवान् निन्रनवुम्
तीयिनाल् तूशागुं चेप्पेलोरेम्पावाय् ॥

Māyanai mannu vaḍamadurai maindanai,
Tūya perunīr yamunaitturaivanai,
Āyar kulattinil tónṛum aṇiviḷakkai
Tāyaik kudalviḷakkam śeida Dāmodaranai
Tūyomāi vantu nām tūmalar tūvittozhudu
Vāyināl pādi manattinal cindikka
póya pizhaiyum pugutaruvān ninṛanavum
Tīyināl tūśagum céppélo rémpāvāi.

5. If we, pure in our hearts, meditate on,
offer flowers to and sing praises of
the mysterious One, born in North Mathura
residing on the banks of Yamuna, the river
with pure waters, the light of the Gokula clan,
Damodara, who has made his mother's womb radiant,
All sins, past and future, will disappear
like dust in fire.
Let us, therefore, recite His names.

राग : शंकराभरणं Rāga : Sankarabharanam

6. पुळ्ळुं शिलंबिनकाण्; पुळ्ळरैयन् कोयिलिल्
वेळ्ळै विळिशंखिन् पेररवं केट्टिलैयो?
पिळ्ळाय्! येलुन्तिराय्, पेय्मुलै नञ्चुण्डु,
कळ्ळच्चकडं कलक्कलि़यक् कालोच्चि,
वेळ्ळत्तरविल् तुयिलमर्न्द वित्तिनै,
उळ्ळत्तुक्कोण्डु मुनिवर्गळुं योगिकळुम्
मेळ्ळ येलुन्दु अरियेन्र पेररवम्
उळ्ळं पुगुन्दु कुळिर्न्देलोरेम्पावाय् ॥

Puḷḷum śilambinkāṇ; puḷḷaraiyan kóyilil
Véḷḷai viḷisánkhin péraravam kéttilaiyo?
Pillāi yézhuntirāi, péymulai nancundu,
Kaḷḷaccakadam kalakkazhiyakkālocci,
Véllattaravil tūyilamarnda vittinai,
Uḷḷattukkondu munivargalum yogikalum
Méḷḷa yézhundu ariyénḍra péraravam
Uḷḷam pugundu kulirndélo rémpāvāi.

6. The birds have started chirping.
Don't you hear the sound of the sacred white conch
from the temple of our Lord, whose vehicle
is the king of birds (*Garuda*)?
Child! get up!
Doesn't the chanting of the words "Hari! Hari",
of the sages and Yogis (who have meditated on
the Lord who is resting on the white milky ocean,
who sucked the poison on the breasts of the devilish
Pootana,* along with her life, and who broke to pieces
the cart which came at high speed**),
get into you and cool your heart?
Please get up!

*THE POOTANA EPISODE

Pootana was a ruthless demoness sent by the evil Kamsa to kill infant Krishna. She went to Gokula, disguised as a beautiful woman, took Krishna on her lap and suckled him. Her breasts were poisoned to kill Krishna, but Krishna sucked and drained not only the poison but her life breath as well. Destruction of Pootana, the demoness, is one of the famous miracles performed by child Krishna.

**DESTRUCTION OF CART WHEEL DEMON

Kamsa sent another demon to kill Krishna, disguised as a cart. Infant Krishna with his tiny, tender legs kicked the cart, broke it into pieces and destroyed the demon.

राग : भैरवि

Rāga : Bhairavi

7. कीचु कीचेन्रेङ्गुं आनैच्चात्तन् कलन्दु
पेशिन पेच्चरवं केट्टिलैयो ? पेय् प्पेण्णे !
काशुं पिऱ्प्पुं कलकलप्पक्कैपेर्त्तु
वाश नरुंकुऴल् आय्च्चियर् मत्तिनाल
ओशैप्पडुत्त त्तयिररवं केट्टिलैयो ?
नायकप्पेण्पिळ्ळाय् ! नारायणन्मूर्त्ति
केशवनैप्पाडवुं नी केट्टे किडत्तियो ?
तेश मुडैयाय् ! तिऱ्वेलो रेम्पावाय् ।।

Kīcu kīcendréngum ānaiccattan kalandu
peśina péccaravam kéṭṭilaiyo? péy pénné!
Kāśum piṛappum kalakalappakkai pérttu
Vāśa naṛunkuzhal āycchiyar mattināl
Ośaippaḍutta ttayiraravam kéṭṭilaiyo?
Nāyakappénpillāi! Nārāyaṇanmūrti
Kéśavanāip pāḍavum nī kéṭṭé kiḍattiyo?
Tésamudaiyāi! tiravélorémpāvāi.

7. O! Senseless girl! Haven't you heard yet
the screeching sound of the birds' chirping?
Haven't you heard the sound of the cowherdesses'
churning curds, wearing fragrant flowers and
jingling bangles on their hands moving forward and backward?
O! Leader of girls! Are you still sleeping, hearing us
singing the glories of Sri *Narayana,* who is also called
*Keshava** (because of his beautiful hair)?
O! Beautiful One! Open the door.

*HOW KRISHNA BECAME KESHAVA

Kesi was a demon and a friend of Kamsa, Krishna's enemy. He came in the form of a horse to Gokula and attacked Krishna. Krishna put his hand in the horse's mouth and strangled the demon to death. Because he killed Kesi, Krishna was hailed by the angels as Kesava.

राग : धन्यासी

Rāga : Dhanyasi

8. कीऴ् वानं वेळ्ळेन्रु, येरुमै शिरुवीडु
मेय्वान् परन्दन काण्; मिक्कुळ्ळ पिळ्ळैगळुम्
पोवान् पोगिन्रारैप्पोगामल् कात्तुन्नै
कूवुवान् वन्दु निन्रों, कोदुकलमुडैय
पावाय्! येलुन्दिराय्; पाडिप्परैकोण्डु
मावाय् पिळन्दानै, मल्लरै माट्टिय
देवादि देवनैच्चेन्रु नां सेवित्ताल्
आवावेन्राराय्न्दरुळेलोरेंपावाय् ॥

Kīzhvānam véḷḷenru, yérumai Śiruvīdu
Méyvān parandana kāṇ; mikkuḷḷa piḷḷaigaḷum
Póvān póginrāraippógāmal kāttunnai
kūvuvān vandu ninrom, kódukalamudaiya
pāvāi yézhundirāi; pādippaṛai kondu
Māvāi piḷandānai, mallarai māṭṭiya
Dévāti dévanai cchendru nām sévittāl
Āvāvénrārāindaruḷélorémpāvai.

8. The lower horizon has become bright.
The buffaloes have gone to graze the dewy grass.
For your sake, we have stopped the others who are ready to go for the ritual bath,
and we are standing at your doorstep.
O! Curious One! Get up!
Let us sing the praises of Sri Krishna
and seek His grace.
If we bow to the Lord of lords, who
slit open the horsefaced demon* and
destroyed the wrestlers, he will
be compassionate and bless us.

*Demon Kesi.

राग : हमीर कल्याणि Rāga : Hamīr Kalyāni

9. तूमणि माडत्तुच्चुट्टं विळक्केरिय
तूपंकमऴत्तुयिलणैमेल् कण्वळरुम्
मामान्मकळे ! मणिक्कतवं ताळ् तिरवाय्
मामीर् ! अवळै येलुप्पीरो ? उम्मगळ्तान्
ऊमैयो ? अन्रिच्चेविडो अनन्दलो ?
येमप्पेरुन्दुयिल् मन्दिरप्पट्टाळो
"मामायन्, माधवन्, वैकुण्ठन्" येन्रेन्रु
नामं पलवुं नविन्रेलो रेम्पावाय् ॥

Tūmaṇi māḍattucchutrum viḷakkériya
Tūpam kamazhattuyilaṇai mél kaṇvaḷarum
Māmān makalé! maṇikkatavam tāḷtiravāi
Māmīr! avaḷai yezhuppīro? ummagaltān
Ūmaiyo? anricchévido anandalo?
Yémappérunduyil mandirappaṭṭāḷo
"Māmāyan, mādhavan, vaikuṇṭan" énrénru
Nāmam palavum navinrélo rempāvāi.

9. While the lights burn in the
diamond studded palaces,
You uncle's daughter!, who sleep
on the soft bed, open the door bolts.
Auntie! Is your daughter deaf and dumb?
Or is she unconscious?
Is she sunk in deep slumber that she cannot get up?
Even after we have chanted the names of the Lord:
"O! Mysterious One!, O! Madhava, the Lord of Lakshmi!,
O! Resident of Vaikunta!", she has not come out.
Please wake up your daughter!

राग : तोडि

Rāga : Todi

10. नोट्रुच्चुवर्गं पुगुकिऩ्र अंमनाय्!
माट्रमुं तारारो वाशल् तिऱवादार्?
नाट्रत्तुऴाय्मुडि नारायणऩ्म्माल्
पोट्रप्पऱै तरुं पुण्णियऩाल् पण्डोरुनाळ्
कूट्रत्तिऩ् वाय् वीलून्द कुंबकरणनुम्
तोट्रुं उनक्के पेरुन्दुयिल् ताऩ् तन्तानो?
आट्र अनन्तल् उडैयाय्! अरुंकलमे!
तेट्रमाय् वन्दु तिऱवेलो रेम्पावाय्॥

Noṭruccuvargam pugukinṛa ammanāi!
Māṭramum tarāro vāśal tiṛavādār?
Nāṭrattuzhāimudi Nārāyaṇannammāl
Poṭrapparai tarum punniyanāl pandorunāḷ
Kūṭrattin vāi vīzhnda kumbakaraṇanum
Totrum unakké pérunduyil tān tantāno?
Āṭra anantal uḍaiyāi! arunkalamé!
Tétramāi vandu tiravélo rempāvāi.

10. O! Girl, who has tasted heaven by performing the ritual!
Even though you have not opened the door,
Can you not at least vocally respond to our call?
Lord Narayana, who wears a crown of fragrant Tulasi leaves
is the Holy Deity who will bless us.
Has Kumbhakarna, who in the past fell into Yama's mouth
bequeathed his sleeping prowess to you?
You, Lazy One! Unique Gem!
Clear your senses and come and open the door.

राग : हुसेनी Rāga : Huseni

11. कट्ुक्कऱ्वैक्कणंगळ् पलकऱन्दु
शेट्रार्तिऱलल़ियच्च्वेन्रु शेरुच्च्वेय्युम्
कुट्रमोन्रिल्लाद कोवलर्तं पोऱ्कोडिये !
पुट्ररवल् गुल् पुन मयिले ! पोदराय्,
शुट्रत्तुत्तोल़िमार् येल्लारुं वन्दु निन्
मुट्रं पुकुन्दु मुगिल्वण्णनं पेर्पाड,
शिट्रादे पेशादे शेल्वप्पेण्डाट्टि नी
येट्ु क्कुऱंगुं पोरुळेलो रेंपावाय् ॥

Kaṭṛukkaṛavaik kaṇangal palakaṛandu
Śéṭṛārtiṛalazhiyacchénru śérucchéyyum
Kuṭramonrillāda kovalartam poṛkoḍiyé!
Puṭṛaravalgul punamayilé! podarāi,
Śuṭṛattuttozhimār yéllārum vandu nin
Muṭṛam pukundu mugilvaṇṇan pérpāda,
Śiṭṛādé péśādé śélvappeṇḍāṭṭi nī
Yéṭṛukkuṛangum poruḷélo rémpāvāi.

11. O! Golden Creeper of the clan of blameless cowherds,
who have milked countless cows with calves,
and who have gone and fought bravely evil ones
and destroyed their strength!
You who roam free like a peacock, in the forest!
Get up and come!
All the maids in the neighbourhood have come
to your doorstep and are singing the names of
Cloudhued Sri Krishna.
Yet you are sleeping, silent and motionless.
Why are you behaving like this?

राग : केदारगौल

Rāga : Kedargowla

12. कनैत्तिळं कट्रेरुमै कन्रुक्किरंगि
निनैत्तु मुलैवऴियॆ निन्रु पाल् शोर
ननैत्तिल्लं शेऱाक्कुं नर्चोल्वन् तंगाय्!
पनित्तलै वीऴ् निन्वाशल् कडैपट्रि
चिनत्तिनाल् तेन्निलंगैक्कोमानैच्चेट्र
मनत्तुक्किनियानै प्पाडवुं नी वाय् तिऱवाय्!
इनित्तान् येऴुन्दिराय्; ईदेन्न पेरुरक्कम्?
अनैत्तिल्लत्तारुं अऱिन्देलो रेम्पावाय्॥

Kanaittilam kaṭrérumai kanrukkirangi
Ninaittu mulaivazhiyé ninru pāl śora
Nanaittillam śéṛākkum naṛcolvan tangāi!
Panittalai vīzha ninvāśal kadai paṭri
Cinattināl tennilangaik komānaiccéṭra
Manattukkiniyānaippādavum nī vai tiravāi!
Inittān yézhundirāi; īdénna péruṛakkam?
Anaittillattārum aṛindélo rémpāvāi.

12. O! Sister of the rich One, who owns
buffaloes who wet the house dirty
with the profuse oozing of milk from their udders
in remembrance of their calves,
even though we are standing in front of your home,
the dew falling on our heads,
and singing the praises of Sri Rama,
the darling of our hearts, who destroyed
the Ruler of Sri Lanka in the south,
You are not opening your mouth.
Why don't you get up? What is this great slumber?
Everyone in the neighbourhood has woken up.

राग : अटाना

Rāga : Atānā

13. पुळ्ळिन्वाय् कीण्डानै, पोल्ला अरक्कनै
क्किळ्ळिक् कळैन्दानै क्कीर्त्तिमै पाडिप्पोय्,
पिळ्ळैगळ् येल्लारुं पावैक्कळंपुक्कार्;
वेळ्ळि येलुन्दु, वियाल़ं उऱंगिट्टु;
पुळ्ळुं शिलंबिनकाण्; पोदरिक्कण्णिनाय्!
कुळ्ळक्कुळिरक्कुडैन्दु नीराडादे,
पळ्ळिक्किडत्तियो ? पावाय्! नी नन्नाळाल्
कळ्ळं तविर्न्दु कलन्देलो रेंपावाय्॥

Puḷḷinvāi kiṇḍānai, pollā arakkanaik
Kiḷḷik kaḷaindānaik kīrttimai pādippoy,
Piḷḷaigaḷ yéllārum pāvaikkalampukkar;
Veḷḷi ezhundu, viyāzham uṛangitru;
Puḷḷum śilambinakāṇ; podarikkaṇṇināi!
Kuḷḷak kuḷirak kuḍaindu nīraḍādé,
Paḷḷik kiḍattiyo? Pāvāi! nī nannaḷāl
Kaḷḷam tavirndu kalandélo rémpāvāi.

13. Singing the praises of the Lord,
who slit open the mouth of the demon Baka*
who came in the shape of a bird,
and who clipped away the ten heads of Ravana,
all the other girls have gone for the ritual.
Venus has risen, Jupiter has set.
The birds have begun their chirping
O! Girl with beautiful eyes like the lotus and the gazelle!
O! doll like beauty!
On this auspicious day,
Give up the ruse of thinking of Krishna alone
and mingle with us in the bath ritual.
Is it right to still lie in bed?

*Demon Baka, Pootana's brother, came in the form of a crane one day when Krishna and his companions were drinking water from the Yamuna river, and attacked Krishna. Krishna tore apart the two beaks of the crane and destroyed the demon.

राग : आनन्दभैरवि

Rāga : Anandabhairavi

14. उंगळ् पुऴ़ैक्कडै त्तोट्टत्तु वावियुळ्
शेंगऴुनीर् वाय् नेगिऴ़्न्दु आंबल्वाय् कूंबिनकाण्;
शेंगल् पोडिक्कूऱै वेण्बल् तवत्तवर्,
तंगळ् तिरुक्कोयिल् शंखिडुवान् पोगिन्ऱार्;
येंगळै मुन्नं येऴुप्पुवान् वाय् पेशुम्
नंगाय्! येऴुन्दिराय्, नाणादाय्! नावुडैयाय्!
शंखोडु शक्करं येन्दुं तडक्कैयन्
पंगयक्कण्णानै प्पाडेलो रेंपावाय्॥

Ungaḷ puzhaikkadait toṭṭattu vāviyuḷ
Śéngazhunīr vāi négizhndu āmbalvāi kūmbinakāṇ;
Śéngal podikkūrai vénbal tavattavar,
Tangal tirukkoyil śankhiduvān poginrar;
Yéngaḷai munnam ézhuppuvān vāi péśum
Nangāi! yezhundirāi, nāṇādāi! nāvudaiyāi!
Śankhoḍu śakkaram yéndum tadakkaiyan
Pangayakkaṇṇānai ppādélo rémpāvāi.

14. The red lotuses, in your backyard garden pond have bloomed.
The blue lotuses (which bloom only at night) have folded up.
The sages are going to the temple to blow the conch and wake up the Lord.
Girl! You pompously promised to wake us up!
Not only did you not get up, you are shameless and silent.
Come quickly! Let us sing the glory of Sri Krishna
who holds in his long divine hands the discus and the conch.

राग : बेगडा Rāga : Begada

15. येल्ले इऴंकिऴिये! इन्नं उऱंगुदियो?
चिल्लेन्ऱऴैयेन्मिन्, नंगैमीर पोदर्किन्रेन्;
'वल्लै, उन् कट्टुरैक्ळ! पण्डे उन् वायऱिदुम्!'
'वल्लीर्गळ् नींगळे, नानेतान् आयिडुग!'
'ओल्लै नी पोदाय, उनक्केन्न वेऱुडैयै?'
'येल्लोरुं पोन्तारो?' 'पोन्तार्, पोन्तु येण्णिक्कोळ्'
वल्लानै कोन्ऱानै, माट्रारै माट्रऴिक्क
वल्लानै, मायनै प्पाडेलो रेम्पावाय्॥

Yéllé iḷankiḷiyé! innam uṛangudiyo?
Cillénṛazhaiyénmin, nangaimīr! podarkinrén;
'Vallai, un kaṭṭuraikal! pandé un vāyaṛidum!'
'Vallīrgal nīngalé, nānétān āyiḍuga!'
'Ollai nī podāi, unakkénna véṛudaiyai?'
'Ellorum pontāro?' 'pontār, pontu eṇṇikkol'
Vallānai konṛānai, māṭṛārai mātrazhikka
Vallānaị māyanai ppādélo rémpāvāi.

15. "O! Sweetie Bird! Are you still sleeping?"
"Girls! Don't shout. I am just coming"
"We know well your valour of words!"
"You are all good at your words. Let it be so."
"What is so special about you? First you come."
"Has everybody come?"
"Yes. If necessary, you come and count"
Let us go singing the glory of Krishna,
who killed the great elephant Kuvalaya Peetha
and destroyed the might of the demons.

राग : दरबार / मोहनम्                                   Rāga : Durbar/Mohanam

16. नायकनाय् नित्र नन्दगोपनुडैय
कोयिल् काप्पाने ! कोटित्तोन्रुं तोरण
वायिल् काप्पाने ! मणिक्कदवं ताळ्तिऱ्वाय्;
आयर् शिऱुमियरोमुक्कु अऱै पऱै
मायन् मणिवण्णन् नेन्नले वाय् नेन्दान्;
तूयोमाय् वन्तोम् तुयिलेऴ्प्पाडुवान्;
वायाल् मुन्नमुन्नं माट्राद अंमा ! नी
नेय निलैक्कदवं नीक्कलो रेंपावाय् ॥

Nayakanāi ninra nandagopanudaiya
Koil kāppāné! kotittonrum torana
Vāyil kāppāné! maṇikkadavam tāltiravai;
Āyar śirumiyaromukku aṛai paṛai
Māyan manivannan nénnalé vāi nérndān;
Tūyomāi vantom tūyilézhappāḍuvan;
Vāyāl munnamunnam māṭṛādé ammā! nī
Néya nilaikkadavam nīkkalo rémpāvāi.

16. O! Guard of Nandagopa's palace!
O! Keeper of the gate, adorned with flags and festoons!
Open the bolts of the door!
Sri Krishna has already promised yesterday
to give us our boons. Pure in our hearts,
We have come to sing His praises and wake Him up
to get our boons.
Don't refuse us; please let us in.

राग : कल्याणि

Rāga : Kalyāni

17. अंबरमे, तण्णीरे, शोऱे अऱञ्चेय्युम्
येंपेरुमान्! नन्दगोपाला! येऴुन्दिराय;
कोंबनार्क्केल्लां कोऴुन्दे! कुलविळक्के!
येंपेरुमाट्टि! यशोदाय् अऱिवुऱाय्;
अंबरं ऊंडरुत्तोंगि उलगलन्द
उम्बर्कोमाने! उऱंगादेऴुन्दिराय्;
शेंपोर्कऴलडिच्चेल्वा! बलदेवा!
उंबियुं नीयुं उऱंगेलोरेंपावाय्॥

Ambaramé, taṇṇīré, śoré aṛancéyyum
Empérumān! Nandagopālā! yézhundirāi;
Kombanārkkellām kozhundé! kulaviḷakké!
Émpérumāṭṭi! Yasodāi! aṛivaṛāi;
Ambaram ūnduṛuttongi ulagalanda
Umbarkomāné! uṛangādezhundirāi;
Śémpoṛkazhalaḍiccélvā! Baladévā!
Umbiyum nīyum uṛangélorempāvāi.

17. O! Nandagopa! O! Chief! Who gives food, clothes and water to the satisfaction of all! Wake up!

O! Mother Yasoda! Womankind's Jewel! Light of the family! Wake up!

O! Lord of lords who measured the worlds,

spanning the skies! Wake up!

O! Balarama! You and your younger brother Krishna

please wake up from sleep and bless us.

राग : सहाना Rāga : Sahāna

19. कुत्तु विळक्केरियक्कोट्टुक्काल् कट्टिल्मेल्
मेत्तेन्र पञ्च शयनत्तिन् मेलेऱि
कोत्तल पूंकुऴल् नप्पिन्नै कोंगै मेल्
वैत्तुक्किडन्द मलर्मार्पा ! वाय् तिऱवाय्;
मैत्तडंकण्णिनाय्! नी उन् मणाळनै
येत्तनै पोतुं तुयिलेऴ ओट्टाय्काण्,
येत्तनै येलुं पिरिवाट्र किल्लायाल्,
तत्तुवं अन्रु तकवेलो रेंपावाय् ॥

Kuttu vilakkériyak koṭṭukkāl kaṭṭilmél
Métténra panca śayanattin méléṛi
kottalar pūnkuzhal nappinnai kongaimél
Vaittuk kiḍanda malar mārpā! vāi tiravāi;
Maittadankaṇṇināi! nī un maṇāḷanai
Éttanai potum tuyilézha oṭṭāikāṇ,
éttanaiyélum pirivāṭra killāyāl,
tattuvam anṛu takavélor émpāvāi.

19. The lamps burn all around
On the cot, supported by ivory legs,
You sleep on the bosom of Niladevi
You broad chested Lord!
Why don't you speak a word?
O! Goddess, whose eyes are beautiful with collyrium,
you will not allow your husband to get up, whatever the time,
You don't want to be separated from Him even for a moment.
Is this proper?

राग : चेञ्चुरिटी Rāga : Chenchurutti

20. मुप्पत्तु मूवर् अमरर्क्कु मुन् शेन्रु
कप्पं तविर्क्कुं कलिये! तुयिलेऴाय्;
शेप्पं उडैयाय्! तिर्लुडैयाय्! शेट्रार्क्कु
वेप्पं कोडुक्कुं विमला! तुयिलेऴाय्:
चेप्पन्न मेन्मुलै चेव्वाय् शिरुमरुंगुल्
नप्पिन्नै नंगाय्! तिरुवे! तुयिलेऴाय्;
उक्कमुं तट्टोळियुं तन्तुन् मणाळनै
इप्पोदे येम्मै नीराट्टेलो रेंपावाय्॥

Muppattu mūvar amorarkku mun śénru
Kappam tavirkkum kaliyé! tuyilézhāi;
Śéppam uḍāiyāy! tiṛaludaiyāy! śétrārkku
Véppam kodukkum vimala! tuyilézhāi;
Céppanna ménmulai cevvāi śiṛumarungul
Nappinnai nangāi! tiruvé! tuyilézhāi;
Ukkamum taṭṭoḷiyum tantun maṇāḷanāi
Ippodé yemmāi nīrāttélo répāvāi.

20. O! Ocean of mercy!
Who wipes away the sorrow of thirty-three crores of angels
Wake up from your slumber!
You have the strength to protect your devotees
and destroy evil, You Stainless One!
Wake up!
O! Beautiful Niladevi! Wake up!
Give us the mirror and the fan for the ritual
and send us for our bath.

राग : नादनामक्रिया

Rāga : Nādanāmakriyā

21. यैट्र् कलंगळ् येदिर्पोंगि मीदळिप्प
मात्रादे पाल् शोरियुं वळ्ळऱ् पेरुंपशुक्कळ्
आट्रप्पडैत्तान् मकने! अऱिवुऱाय्;
ऊट्रं उडैयाय्! पेरियाय्! उलकिनिल्
तोट्रमाय् निन्र शुडरे! तुयिलेऴाय्;
माट्ररा उनक्कु वलितोलैन्दुन् वाशऱ्कण्
आट्रादु वन्तुन् अडिपणियुमाप्पोले,
पोट्रियां वन्तों पुगऴ्न्देलोरेंपावाय्॥

Yéṭra kalangal édirpongi mīdaḷippa
Mātrādé pāl śoriyum vaḷḷaṛ perumpaśukkaḷ
Ātrappadaittān makané! aṛivuṛāi;
Ūtram udaiyāi! periyāi! ulakinil
Toṭramāi ninra śudaré! tuyilézhāi;
Māṭrarā unakku valitolaindun vāśaṛkaṇ
Ātrādu vantun adipaṇiyumāppolé,
Potriyām vantom pugazhndélorempāvāi.

21. O! Son of Nandagopa,
who has big cows which overfill the pitchers
placed under their udders with milk,
Wake up!
O! Strong One! O! Great One! O! Radiant One!
Wake up!
Like the enemies who come to your doorstep and seek refuge in you,
we also have come, praising you, to you.

राग : यमुनाकल्याणी

Rāga : Yamunākalyānī

22. अंगण् मा ज्ञालत्तरशर् अभिमान
भंगमाय् वन्दुनिन् पळ्ळिक्कट्टिऱ्कीऴे
शंगम् इरुप्पार्पोल वन्तु तलैप्पेय्दोम्;
किंगिणि वाय्च्चेय्द तामरैप्पूप्पोले,
शेंगण शिरुच्चिरिदे येम्मेल् विऴियावो ?
तिंगळुं आदित्यनुं येऴुन्दार्प्पोल,
अंगणिरण्डुं कोण्डेंगळ् मेल् नोक्कुदियेल्
येंगळ मेल् शापं इऴिन्देलो रेंपावाय्॥

Anganmā jnālattaraśar abhimāna
Bhangamāi vandu nin pallikkaṭṭiṛkīzhé
Śangam iruppārpol vantu talaippéydom;
Kingiṇi vāiccéyda tāmaraippūppolé,
Séngaṇ śiṛucciridé yémmél vizhiyāvo?
Tingaḷum ādittiyanum yezhundāṛpol,
Angaṇirandunkondéngal mél nokkudiyél
Yéngaḷmél śāpam izhindélo rémpāvāi.

22. Just as various rulers, their arrogance humbled,
wait in clusters, by your bedside,
We also have come to you.
Can't your kind glance, resembling the slightly open lotus,
fall on us?
Once you see us with your eyes, like the rise of the sun and the moon, all our afflictions will be over.

राग : मणिरंगु / बिलहरी Rāga : Manirangu/Bilahari

23. मारि मलै मुऌ़ैञ्चिल् मन्निक्किडन्तुऱंगुम्
शीरिय शिंगं अऱिवुट्ट्रु त्तीविऴित्तु,
वेरि मयिर् पोंग येप्पाडुं पेर्न्दुदऱि,
मूरि निमिर्न्दु मुऴंगि प्पुऱप्पट्टु
पोदरुमा पोले नी पूवैप्पूवण्णा ! उन्
कोयिल् निन्रिङ्गने पोन्दरुळिक्कोप्पुडैय
शीरिय शिंगाशनत्तिरुन्दु यां वन्द
कारियं आरायुन्दरुळेलोरेंपावाय् ॥

Māri malaimuzhaincil mannikkidanturangum
Śīriya śingam arivutruttīvizhittu,
Véri mayir ponga yeppādum pérndudaṛi,
Mūri nimirndu muzhangi ppuṛappattu
Podarumā polé nī pūvaippūvaṇṇā! un
Koil ninringané pondaruḷikkoppudaiya
Śīriya śingāśanattirundu yām vanda
Kāriyam ārāindaruḷélorempāvāi.

23. During the rainy season,
the lion sleeps in the mountain den,
thereafter it wakes up and comes out
eyes flashing fire, and roaring.
Likewise, You also come out of your den, ascend the throne
and listen to our pleadings and bless us, O! Bluehued One!
(Whose blue colour is like that of the blue lotus!).

राग : सिन्धुभैरवि

Rāga : Sindhubhairavi

24. अन्रिव्वुलगं अळन्ताय्! अडि पोट्रि,
शेन्रंगुत्तेन्निलंगै शेट्राय्! तिऱल् पोट्रि,
पोन्रच्चकटं उदैत्ताय! पुकऴ् पोट्रि,
कन्रु कुणिला येरिन्दाय्! कऴल् पोट्रि,
कुन्रु कुडैया येडुत्ताय्! गुणं पोट्रि,
वेन्रु पगै केडुक्कुं निन् कैयिल् वेल् पोट्रि,
येन्रेन्रुं शेवगमे येत्तिप्पऱैकोळ्वान्
इन्रु यां वन्तों, इरंगेलोरेंपावाय्॥

Anṛivvulagam aḷantai! adi potri,
Śénṛanguttennilangai śetrāi! tiṛal potri,
Ponraccakaṭam udaittāi! pukazh potri,
Kanṛu kuṇila yéṛindāi! kazhal potri,
Kunṛu kudaiyāi yéduttāi! guṇam potri,
Venṛu pagai kédukkum nin kaiyil vél potri,
Énrénrum śévagamé yéttipaṛai koḷvān
Inru yām vantom, irangélorémpāvāi.

24. Years ago, You measured all the worlds with your feet.
Hail Your holy feet!
You went to Sri Lanka and destroyed the demons.
Hail Your valour!
You broke to pieces the demon Sakata!* Hail your fame!
You threw the demon calf!** (against the demon tree)
Hail your prowess!
You held the mountain as umbrella!*** Hail your goodness!
Hail the spear in your hands which conquers and destroys evil.
We have come to sing your praises, ever your servants,
Please be compassionate to us.

*The cart wheel demon.

**One day when Krishna was herding the calves, a demon came in the disguise of a calf. Krishna recognised the demon, caught the calf by the hindleg and threw it dead against the top of a tree.

***Once Krishna made Indra, the Chief of angels, angry, by stopping a sacrifice in his honour. Indra felt insulted and decided to punish Krishna and the cowherds by sending down torrential rain. The cowherds panicked and collected around Krishna, who uprooted the Govardhana mountain with his arms and held it aloft like an umbrella, while the cowherds and their belongings and cows stood protected from the rainwater, under the soft and sandy bed of the mountain.

Indra poured down heavy rain for seven days and nights, but Krishna did not flinch and Indra had to retreat in defeat.

After this episode Krishna came to be called affectionately: Giridhari, the Holder of the mountain.

राग : बेहाग

Rāga : Béhāg

25. ओरुत्ति मकनाय्प् पिऱन्तु, ओरिरविल्
ओरुत्ति मकनाय् ओळित्तु वळर,
तरिक्किलानागि त्तान् तीङ्गु निनैन्द
करुत्तैप्पिऴैप्पित्तु क्कंशन् वयिट्रिल्
नेरुप्पेन्न निन्र नेडुमाले! उन्नै
अरुत्तित्तु वन्तों; पऱैतरुदियागिल्
तिरुत्तक्क शेल्वमुं शेवगमुं यां पाडि
वरुत्तमुं तीन्र्दु मकिऴ्न्देलोरेंपावाय्।

Orutti makanāip piṛantu, óriravil
Orutti makanāi oḷittu vaḷara
Tarikkilānāgittān tīngu ninainda
Karuttaip pizhaippittuk kamśan vayitril
Neruppénna ninṛa nédumālé! unnai
Aruttittu vantom; paṛai tarudiyāgil
Tiruttakka śélvamum śévagamum yām pādi
Varuttamum tīrndu makizhndélo rempāvāi.

25. Born to one woman, the same night
you became another woman's son,*
and grew up in secrecy,
You put an end to the evil intentions of Kamsa
who wanted to kill you, out of envy,
and became the fire in his stomach, O! Lord!
We have come seeking you.
With your grace,
we shall have all that we want
and shall be happy, without any want.

*Krishna was born as the child of Devaki and Vasudeva, kept captives by the evilminded Kamsa, Devaki's brother. To save the newborn child from destruction by Kamsa, Vasudeva was directed by Divine guidance to take Krishna to Nandagopa's house across the river Kalindi, where Yasoda, Nandagopa's wife, had just delivered a daughter, and interchange the newborn babies. Accordingly Vasudeva took Krishna in his hands and proceeded on a stormy night to Gokula. During the journey, newborn Krishna was protected from the rain by the serpent Adisesha and Vasudeva safely completed the mission and returned home with Yasoda's daughter, the Divine forces ensuring open doors everywhere and sleeping attendants during the operation.

Thus it is that Andal refers to Krishna as having been born to one woman and becoming another woman's son the same night.

राग : कुन्तालवराृलि

Rāga : Kuntālavarāli

26. माले मणिवण्णा ! मार्गलि़ नीराडुवान्
मेलैयार् शेय्वनगळ् वेण्डुवन केट्टियेल्
ज्ञालत्तै येल्लां नडुंग मुरल्वन
पालन्न वण्णत्तुन् पाञ्चजन्यमे
पोल्वन शंखंगळ् पोय्प्पाडुडैयनवे,
शालप्पेरुंपरैये, पल्लाण्डिशैप्पारे
कोलविळक्के, कोडिये, विधानमे,
आलिन् इलैयाय् ! अरुळेलोरेंपावाय् ॥

Mālé manivaṇṇā! mārgazhi nīrāḍuvān
Mélaiyār śéyvanagal véṇḍuvana kéṭṭiyél
Gnālattai ẹllām nadunga muralvana
Pālanna vaṇṇattun pānca janniyamé
Pólvana śankhangal poyppāḍudaiyanavé
Śālappérum paraiyé, pallāndisaippāré
Kolaviḷakké, kodiyé, vidhānamé,
Ālin ilaiyāi! aruḷélorémpāvāi.

26. O! Lord, who love us!
Bluehued One! (Whose colour is like that of the blue sapphire.)
Who resides in the leaf of the banyan tree!
For the Margasirsa month ritual, to be observed
in the tradition of our ancestors,
we hereby list our demands:
Conches like your Panchajanya,
drums which can resoundingly proclaim your greatness,
clusters of devotees like us,
beautiful lamps, flags and festoons.
Be pleased to grant these.

राग : पूर्वकल्याणि Rāga : Poorvakalyāni

27. कूडारै वेल्लुं शीर्गोविन्दा! उन्तन्नै
पाडिप्परै कोण्डु यां पेरुं सम्मानम्;
नाडु पुकलुं परिशिनाल् नन्राग,
शूडगमे तोळ्वळैये तोडे शेविप्पूवे
पाडगमे येन्रनैय पल्कलनुं यां अणिवोम्;
आडै उडुप्पों; अदन् पिन्ने पारुचोरु
मूड नेय् पेयदु मुलंगै वलि वार
कूडियिरुन्दु कुळिन्र्देलो रेंपावाय्॥

Kūdārai Vellum Śīrgovinda! untannai
Pādipparai kondu yām peṛum sammānam;
Nādu pukazhum pariśināl nanṛaga,
Śūdagamé tolvalaiyé todé śévippūvé
Pādagamé énṛanaiya palkalanum yām aṇivom;
Ādai uḍuppom; adan pinné pāṛcoru
Mūda néypéydu muzhangai vazhi vāra
Kūḍiyirundu kuḷirndélo rémpāvāi.

27. O! Govinda! Protector of the cows!
who triumph over evil ones!
We shall sing your glories and get as our prize:
universal acclaim,
We shall wear various ornaments:
bangles for our hands,
ear-rings, anklets etc,
and good clothes and enjoy ourselves
eating, all together, rice pudding,
dripping with ghee.
We shall complete the ritual, singing your glory.

राग : कांबोजी

Rāga : Kāmboji

28. कऱवैगळ् पिन्शेन्नु कानं शेन्दु उण्बोम्
अऱिवोन्नुं इल्लात आय्क्कुलत्तु उन्तन्नै
पिऱवि पेऱुन्दनै प्पुण्यं यां उडैयोम्;
कुऱैवोन्नुं इल्लात गोविन्दा! उन् तन्नोडु
उऱवेल् नमक्किङ्ङोऴिक्क ओऴियादु!
अऱियात पिळ्ळैगळों अन्पिनाल् उन्नन्नै
चिऱुपेर् अऴैत्तनवुं शीऱि अरुळादे,
इऱैवा, नी ताराय् पऱैयेलो रेंपावाय्॥

Kaṛavaigal pinśénṛu kānam śérndu unbom
aṛivonṛum illāta āykkulattu untannai
piṛavi pérundanaippunniyam yām udaiyom;
Kuṛavonṛum illāta Govindā! un tannodu
uṛavél namakkinkozhikka ozhiyādu!
Aṛiyāta piḷḷaigaḷóm anpināl unrannai
Ciṛupér azhaittanavum śīṛi aruḷādé,
Iṛaivā, nī tārāi paṛaiyélo rémpāvāi.

28. We shall go after the cows and
eat in the forests;
How blessed we are in getting you for our clan
(not very literate or knowledgeable),
O! Stainless Govinda! Protector of cows!
No one can destroy this relationship between you and us;
In our ignorance, out of our love for you,
we have called you by inappropriate names,
Forgive us, don't be angry.
O! God! Be gracious to us.

राग : मलयमारुतम्/मध्यमावती Rāga : Malayamarutam/Madhyamavati

29. शिट्रं शिऱु काले वन्तुन्नैच् चेवित्तुन्
पोट्रामरै यडिये पोट्टुं पोरुळ् केळाय्;
पेट्रं मेय्त्तुण्णुं कुलत्तिल् पिऱन्तु नी
कुट्रेवल् येंगळै क्कोळ्ळामल् पोगादु;
इट्रै प्पऱै कोळ्वान् अन्रुकाण् गोविन्दा!
येट्रैक्कुं येऴेऴ् पिऱविक्कुं उन्तन्नोडु
उट्रोमे आवों; उनक्केनां आट्शेय्वोम्;
मट्रै नं कामंकळ् माट्रेलो रेंपावाय्॥

Śitṛam śiṛu kālé vantunnaic cévittun
Potṛamarai yaḍiyé potrum poruḷ kélāi;
Pétṛam méyttuṇṇum kulattil piṛantu nī
Kutréval éngaḷaik koḷḷāmal pogādu;
Itṛaip paṛai koḷvän anṛukāṇ Govinda!
Étṛaikkum yézhézh piṛavikkum untannódu
Utromé āvom; unakkénām ātśeyvom;
Matrai nam kāmankal mātrélo rémpāvāi.

29. Please ask us why we have come to praise your holy feet, this early morning:
You born in our Yadava clan,
should not refuse to accept us and our offerings.
We have come not for your blessings for today,
Not today, not only in this birth, but in all
future births, we should not deem anything other than you as great,
we should ever be your servants and
do your work, as your instruments.
Let all our other desires be changed to these.
Please bless us!

राग : चुरुट्टी Rāga : Churutti

30. वंगक्कडल् कडैन्द माधवनैक् केशवनै
तिंगळ तिरुमुगत्तुच् चेयिल़ैयार् शेन्रिरैञ्चि
अंगप्परै़कोण्ड आट्रै, अणि पुदुवै
पैंकमलत्तण् तेरियल् बट्टर् पिरान् कोदै शोन्न
शंगत्तमिल़् मालै मुप्पदुं तप्पामे
इंगिप् परिशुरैप्पार्, ईरिरण्डु माल्वरैत्तोळ्
शेंगण् तिरुमुखत्तुच् चेल्वत् तिरुमालाल्
येंगुं तिरुवरुळ् पेट्रिन्पुरुव रेंपावाय्॥

Vangakkaḍal kaḍainda Mādhavanaik Kéśavanai
Tingal tirumugattuccéyizhaiyār śénṛiṛainci
Angappaṛaikonḍa ātṛai, aṇi puduvai
painkamalattaṇ tériyal baṭṭarpirān kodai śonna
Śangattamizhmālai muppadum tappāmé
Ingippariśuraippār, īriranḍu mālvaraittoḷ
Śéngaṇ tirumukhattuc célvattirumālāl
Éngum tiruvaruḷ petṛinpuṛuva rémpāvāi.

30. This story of how the cowherdesses of Gokula
approached and obtained the grace of
Madhava, the Lord of Lakshmi, also known as Kesava,
who churned the milky ocean and gave nectar to the celestial angels,
has been recited by Andal, the daughter of Perialwar,
who wears the garland of lotuses,
in thirty Tamil songs.
Those who recite these regularly
will be blessed by the peerless grace of
the Lord, with the strong shoulders,
red eyes and beautiful face.

# SONGS OF JAYADEVA

*(12th Century A.D.)*

| | *Song* | *Rāga* |
|---|---|---|
| 1. | Jaya Jagadisa Hare | Ragamalika (Bhairavi, Bhoopali, Jayjaywanti, Malkauns, Kedar, Patdeep, Behag, Durga, Poorvadhanyasi, Brindavana sarang, Bhairavi) |
| 2. | Naatha Hare | Charukesi |
| 3. | Saa virahe tava deenaa | Chakravakam |
| 4. | Priye Charuseele | Mukhari |
| 5. | Sakhi He Kesimadana mudaaram | Kalyani |
| 6. | Virahati Haririha | Vasanta |
| 7. | Hari Hari hataadaratayaa | Kharaharapriya |
| 8. | Hari Hari Yaahi Madhava | Bhairavi |
| 9. | Maadhave maa kuru | Poorvakalyani |
| 10. | Yaami he | Nata Bhairavi |

*JAYADEVA*

# JAYADEVA (12th century A.D.)

Few scholars dispute the fact that Jayadeva, the Orissan poet, lived in the 12th century. He was a Sanskrit scholar and poet. A brahmin by birth, he married Padmavati, a dancer. She danced to his songs.

Jayadeva's masterpiece is the *Gīta Govinda,* a poem extolling the love of Radha and Krishna, in erotic imagery.

There are 24 songs in Gīta Govinda. They are called *Ashtapadis,* since each song contains eight stanzas.

The terse beauty of the Sanskrit language, made melodious use of by Jayadeva, invests these songs with musical magic.

These songs inspired Sri Krishna Chaitanya, the great Vaisnavite saint of Bengal. They also inspired the artists of Jammu and Kashmir to evolve a new style of painting called the *Basohli* school of painting.

In the Krishna temple of Guruvayoor in Kerala, Jayadeva's songs are sung daily, set to music in Carnatic ragas.

In Nepal, they are sung during spring celebrations.

The Gīta Govinda of Jayadeva is known as the Indian Song of songs. Sir Edwin Arnold who was one of the first to translate it into English called it: *"The Song Celestial"*.

Two of Jayadeva's songs have been included by Guru Arjun Singh in the Adi Guru Grantha, the holy scripture of the Sikhs.

रागमालिका Rāgamālikā

1. "जय जगदीश हरे"

"Jaya jagadīsa hare"

प्रलय पयोधिजले धृतवानसि वेदम् (भैरवि)
विहित वहित्र चरित्र मखेदम् ।
केशव धृतमीन शरीर जय जगदीश हरे ॥ (जय)

Pralaya payodhijalé dhruthavānasi védam (Bhairavi)
Vihita vahitra caritra makhedam
Kéśava dhrutamīna śarīra jaya Jagadīśa Haré (Jaya)

क्षितिरति विपुलतरे तव तिष्ठति पृष्ठे (भूपालि)
धरणि धरण किण चक्र गरिष्ठे ।
केशव धृत कच्छप रूप जय जगदीश हरे ॥

Kṣitirati vipulataré tava tiṣṭhati pruṣṭhé (Bhoopāli)
Dharaṇi dharaṇa kiṇa cakra gariṣṭhé
Kéśava dhruta kacchapa rūpa jaya Jagadīśa Haré

वसति दशन शिखटे धरणी तव लग्ना (जयजयवन्ति)
शशिनि कलंककलेव निमग्ना ।
केशव धृत शूकर रूप जयजगदीश हरे ॥

Vasati daśana śikharé dharaṇī tava lagna (Jayjaywanti)
Śaśini kalankakaleva nimagnā
Kéśava dhruta śūkara rūpa jaya Jagadīśa Haré

1. *Jaya Jagadīsa Hare!*

In the waters of deluge, You held the Vedas
like a vessel undeflected from its course
O! Kesava! One with beautiful hair! Slayer of the demon Kesi!
You assumed the form of fish!*
Hail Hari! Destroyer of sorrow!
Lord of the universe!

The earth rests on your expansive back
Carrying the heavy earth creates circular marks!
O! Kesava! you assumed the form of tortoise!
Hail Hari! Lord of the universe!

The earth remains on top of your tusk, linked to you
like the blemish mark on the moon.
O! Kesava! You assumed the form of boar!
Hail Hari! Lord of the universe!

तव करकमलवरे नखमद्भुत शृंगम् (मालकौंस)
दलित हिरण्य कशिपु तनु भृंगम्।
केशव धृत नरहरिरूप जय जगदीश हरे॥

Tava karakamalavaré nakhamadbhuta śrungam (Mālkauns)
Dalita hiranya kaśipu tanu bhrungam
Kéśava dhruta naraharirūpa jaya Jagadīśa Haré

छलयसि विक्रमणे बलिमद्भुतवामन (केदार)
पद नख नीरजनितजन पावन।
केशव धृतवामन रूप जय जगदीश हरे॥

Chalayasi vikramané balimadbhuta vāmana (Kedār)
Pada nakha nīrajanitajana pāvana
Kéśava dhruta vāmana rūpa jaya Jagadīśa Haré

क्षत्रिय रुधिर मये जगदपगत पापम् (पटदीप)
स्नपयसि पयसि शमित भव तापम्।
केशव धृत भृगुपतिरूप जय जगदीश हरे॥

Kṣatriya rudhira mayé jagadapagata pāpam (Patdīp)
Snapayasi payasi śamita bhava tāpam
Kéśava dhruta bhrugupati rūpa jaya Jagadīśa Haré

The nails on your lotus hands became wonderful claws
that tore up the body of Hiranyakasipu (demon)
O! Kesava! You assumed the form of man-lion!
Hail Hari! Lord of the universe!

When as the miraculous dwarf, Vamana
You artfully defeated Bali, through your valour
the water dripping from your toenails purified the people!
O! Kesava! You assumed the form of Vamana, the dwarf!
Hail Hari! Lord of the universe!

You bathed the world overcome with sin
in the waters of warrior blood
and put an end to the anguish of the world!
O! Kesava! You assumed the form of Parasurama!
Hail Hari! Lord of the universe!

वितरसि दिक्षु रणे दिक्पति कमनीयम् (बेहाग)
दशमुख मौलि बलिं रमणीयम्।
केशव धृत राम शरीर जय जगदीश हरे॥
Vitaŕasi dikṣu rané dikpati kamanīyam (Behag)
Daśamukha mauli balim ramanīyam
Kéśava dhruta rāma śarīra jaya Jagadīśa Haré

वहसि वपुषि विशदे वसनं जलदाभम् (दुर्गा)
हलहति भीति मिलित यमुनाभम्।
केशव धृत हलधररूप जय जगदीश हरे॥
Vahasi vapuṣi viśadé vasanam jaladābham (Durga)
Halahati bhīti milita yamunābham
Kéśava dhruta haladhara rūpa jaya Jagadīśa Haré

निन्दसि यक्ष विधेरहह श्रुतिजातम् (पूर्वधन्यांसि)
सदय हृदय दर्शित पशु घातम्
केशव धृत बुद्ध शरीर जय जगदीश हरे॥
Nindasi yakṣa vidhérahaha śrutijātam (Poorvadhanyasi)
Sadaya hrudaya darśita paśu ghātam
Kéśava dhruta buddha śarīra jaya Jagadīśa Haré

You scattered the ten heads of Ravana beautifully
in the four directions, rendering the guardians thereof resplendent!
O! Kesava! You assumed the form of Rama!
Hail Hari! Lord of the universe!

You wear on your bright body a raiment
wet with rainwater, mixed with the waters of the Yamuna
flowing as if in fear of your plough!
O! Kesava! You assumed the form of Balarama,
the holder of the plough!
Hail Hari! Lord of the universe!

You criticised demoniac practices born of hearsay
your heart moved by compassion by the sight of a killed animal!
O! Kesava! You assumed the form of Buddha!
Hail Hari! Lord of the universe!

म्लेच्छ निवह निधने कलयसि करवालम् (बृन्दावन सारंग)
धूमकेतुमिव किमपि करालम्।
केशव धृतकल्कि शरीर जय जगदीश हरे॥
Mléccha nivaha nidhané kalayasi karavālam
(Brindāvana Sāranga)

Dhūmaketumiva kimapi karālam
Kéśava dhruta kalki śarīra jaya Jagadīśa Haré

श्री जयदेव कवेरिदमुदित मुदारम् (भैरवि)
शृणु सुखदं शुभदं भवसारम्
केशव धृतदशविध रूप जय जगदीश हरे॥
Śrī jayadéva kavéridamudita mudāram (Bhairavi)
Śruṇu sukhadam śubhadam bhavasāram
Kéśava dhruta dasavidha rūpa jaya Jagadīśa Haré

In the destruction of barbarian hordes,
You swirl your sword like a fierce comet!
O! Kesava! You assume the form of Kalki!
Hail Hari! Lord of the universe!

Listen to this (poem) sung open heartedly
by the poet Jayadeva,
which will bestow happiness, auspiciousness
and contains the essence of creation
O! Kesava! You assumed ten different forms
Hail Hari! Lord of the universe!

*In this prayer reference is made by Jayadeva to the ten incarnations of Vishnu: Fish, Tortoise, Boar, Man-lion, Dwarf (Vamana), Parasurama, Rama, Balarama, Buddha and Kalki. The Krishna incarnation has been omitted, as Krishna has been identified with Vishnu and hence deemed as part of all incarnations.
The various incarnations took place when deluges endangered the cosmos and evil forces threatened the earth, righteousness, the Vedas and the celestial beings.

राग : चारुकेशि

Rāga : Charukeśi

2. नाथ हरे सीदति राधा वासगृहे
पश्यति दिशि दिशि रहसि भवन्तम्
तद धर मधुर मधूनि पबिन्तम् (नाथ हरे)
Nātha haré sīdati Rādhā vāsagruhé
Paśyati diśi diśi rahasi bhavantam
Tad dhara madhura madhūni pibantam (Nātha haré)

त्वदभिसरण रभसेन वलन्ती
पतति पदानि कियन्ती चलन्ती॥ (नाथ हरे)
Twadabhisaraṇa rabhaséna valantī
patati padāni kiyantī calantī (Nātha haré)

विहित विशद बिसकिसलय वलया
जीवति परभिह तव रति कलया (नाथ हरे)
Vihita viśad bisakisalaya valaya
Jīvati parabhiha tava rati kalaya (Nātha haré)

मुहुर वलोकित मण्डनलीला
मधुरिपुरहमिति भावन शीला (नाथ हरे )
Muhura valokita mandanalīlā
Madhuri purahamiti bhāvana śīlā (Nātha hare)

त्वरितमुपैति न कथमभिसारम्
हरिरिति वदति सखीमनुवारम् (नाथ हरे)
Twaritamupaiti na kathamabhisāram
Haririti vadati sakhīmanuvāram (Nātha haré)

श्लिष्यति चुम्बति जलधरकल्पम्
हरिरपगत इति तिमिरमनल्पम् (नाथ हरे)
Śliṣyati cumbati jaladharakalpam
Harirapagata iti timiramanalpam (Nātha haré)

2. *Naatha Haré!*

O! Lord Krishna! Destroyer of sorrow!
In her residence, Radha is pining!
In her solitude, she sees you in every place!
drinking the sweet honeyed lips of others!

In her eagerness to meet you,
She hurries, but falters after a few steps and falls!

Remembering your artful loveplay
through the circlets of tender lotus shoots
She thrives!

O! Krishna, in her residence, Radha is pining.

Repeatedly, looking at the play of her ornaments,
she imagines: "I am Krishna, the Enemy of Madhu!"

How doesn't Krishna come quickly to meet me,
She asks her companions, again and again.

She embraces and kisses dark, cloudlike forms of the night
thinking: "Krishna has come!"

भवति विलम्बिनि विगलितलज्जा
विलपति रोदिति वासक सज्जा (नाथ हरे)
Bhavati vilambini vigalitalajjā
Vilapati roditi vāsaka sajjā (Nātha haré)

श्री जयदेव कवेरिदमुदितम्
रसिक जनं तनुतामतिमुदितम् (नाथ हरे)
Śrī Jayadéva kavéridamuditam
Rasika janam tanutāmatimuditam (Nātha haré)

While you delay,
Giving up her modesty,
She cries and sobs,
all made up to love you!

What has been said here by the poet Sri Jayadeva
Let it give great pleasure to the connoisseurs!

राग : चक्रवाकं Rāga : Chakravākam

3. सा विरहे तव दीना
माधव मनसिज विशिख भयादिव भावनया त्वयि लीना
निन्दति चन्दनमिन्दु किरणमनु विन्दति खेदमधीरम्
व्याल निलय मिलनेन गरलमिव कलयति मलय समीरम् (सा. वि.)
Sā virahé tava dīnā
Mādhava manasija viśikha bhayādiva bhāvanayā twayi līnā
Nindati candanamindu kiraṇamanu vindati khédamadhīram
Vyāla nilaya milanéna garalamiva kalayati malaya samīram
(Sā Vi)

अविरलनिपतित मदनशरादिव भवदवनाय विशालम्
स्वहृदय मर्मणि वर्म करोति सजलनलिनीदलजालम् ॥ (सा. वि.)
Aviralanipatita madana śarādiva bhavadavanāya viśālam
Swahrudaya marmaṇi varma karoti sajalanalini dala jālam
(Sā Vi)

कुसुम विशिख शर तल्पमनल्प विलास कला कमनीयम्
व्रतमिव तव परिरम्भ सुखाय करोति कुसुमशयनीयम् ॥ (सा. वि.)
Kusuma viśikha śara talpamanalp vilāsa kalā kamanīyam
Vratamiva tava pariramhha sukhāya karoti kusumaśayanīyam
(Sā Vi)

वहति च गलित विलोचन जल भरमानन कमलमुदारम्
विधुमिव विकट विधुन्तुददन्तदलन गलिता मृत धारम् ॥ (सा. वि.)
Vahati ca galita vilocana jala bharamānana kamalamudāram
Vidhumiva vikata vidhuntudadantadalana galitā mruta dhāram
(Sā Vi)

विलिखति रहसि कुरङ्गमदेन भवन्तमसम शर भूतम्
प्रणमति मकरमधो विनिधाय करे च शरं नवचूतम् (सा. वि.)
Vilikhati rahasi kurangamadéna bhavantamasama śara bhūtam
Praṇamati makaramadhó vinidhāya karé ca śaram navacūtam
(Sā Vi)

3. *Saa Virahé tava deenaa*

She is pitiable, when separated from you!
O! Madhava! As if afraid of Cupid's arrows,
She is immersed in you!
She hates sandal paste and the rays of the moon,
Sorrow makes her unsteady and weak,
She feels the gentle Southern breeze is like
poison from the nests of deadly serpents!
(She is pitiable, when separated from you!)

As if
To protect you from the incessant fall of Cupid's arrows
She shields the secret recesses of her heart with the
broad, moist petals of the lotus!
(She is pitiable, when separated from you!)

As if to make the bed attractive as a field for the shower of
Cupid's flower arrows,
To enjoy the pleasure of your embrace,
she makes a flower bed as a ritual.
(She is pitiable, when separated from you!)

She wears a face, lotuslike and gentle,
wet with tears from her clouded eyes,
resembling the moon, darkened and cut by the jaws of the
eclipse, oozing nectar!
(She is pitiable, when separated from you!)

In secret, she draws your picture, with deer musk,
in the form of the god of love,
but with a crocodile below you and new mango flowers in
your hands! and then, bows before it.
(She is pitiable, when separated from you!)

प्रतिपदमिदमपि निगदति माधव तव चरणे पतिताहम्
त्वयि विमुखे मयि सपदि सुधानिधिरपि तनुते तनुदाहम् (सा. वि.)
Pratipadamidamapi nigadati Mādhava tava carané patitāham
Tvayi vimukhé mayi sapadi sudhānidhirapi tanuté tanudāham
(Sā Vi)

ध्यानलयेन पुरः परिकल्प्य भवन्तमतीव दुरापम्
विलपति दृसति विषदिति रोदति चञ्चति मुञ्चति तापम् (सा. वि.)
Dhyānalayéna puraha parīkalpya bhavantamatīva durāpam
Vilapati drusati viṣaditi rodati cancati muncati tāpam
(Sā Vi)

श्री जयदेव भणितमिदमधिकं यदि मनसा नटनीयम्
हरि विरहाकुल बल्लवयुवति सखी वचनं पठनीयम् ॥ (सा. वि.)
Śrī Jayadeva bhaṇitamidamadhikam yadi manasā nataniyam
Hari virahākula ballava yuvati sakhī vacanam pathanīyam
(Sā Vi)

Even now, at every step, she cries: "O! Madhava!
I have fallen at your feet!"
"In your absence, even the moon burns my body!"
(She (Radha) is pitiable, when separated from you.)

She invokes you, located so far away, by losing herself in meditation, and cries, laughs, faints, groans, trembles and loses her pain.
(She is pitiable, when separated from you.)

If this song spoken by Sri Jayadeva has to make your heart dance, read the words spoken by Radha's companion, about Radha's condition, when separated from Krishna, the Destroyer of sorrow!

राग : मुखारि Rāga : Mukhāri

4. प्रिये चारुशीले मुञ्च मयि मानमनिदानं
सपदि मदनानलो दहति मम मानसं देहि मुखकमलमधुपानं
वदसि चदि किंचिदपि दन्त रुचि कौमुदी हरति दरतिमिरमतिघोरं
स्फुरदधर सीधवे तव वदन चन्द्रमा रोचयतु लोचन चकोरं (प्रिये)

Priyé cāruśīlé munca mayi mānamanidānam
Sapadi madanānalo dahati mama mānasam déhi mukhakamalamadhupānam
Vadasi cadi kincidapi danta ruci kaumudī harati daratimiramatighoram
Sphuradadhara sīdhavé tava vadana candramā rōcayatu locana cakóram (priyé)

सत्यमेवासि यदि सुदति मयि कोपिनी देहि खरनखरडारघातम्
घटय भुजबन्धनं जनय रदखण्डनं येन वा भवति सुखजातम् (प्रिये)

Satyamévāsi yadi sudati mayi kopinī
déhi kharanakharaḍāraghātam
ghataya bhujabandhanam janaya radakhandanam yéna vā bhavati sukhajātam (priyé)

त्वमसि मम भूषणं त्वमसि मम जीवनं त्वमसि मम भवजलधिरत्नम्
भवतु भवतीह मयि सततमनुरोधिनी तत्र मम हृदय मतियत्नम् (प्रिये)

Twamasi mama bhūṣaṇam twamasi mama jīvanam twamasi mama bhavajaladhiratnam
Bhavatu bhavatīha mayi satatamanurodhinī tatra mama hrudayamatiyatnam (priyé)

नीलनलिना भमपि तन्वि तव लोचनं धारयति कोकनदरूपम्
कुसुम शर बाण भावेन यदि रञ्जयसि कृष्णमिद मेतदनुरूपम् (प्रिये)

Nilanalinā bhamapi tanvi tava locanam
dhārayati kokanadarūpam
Kusuma śara bāna bhāvéna yadi ranjayasi
krisna midamétadanurūpam (priyé)

4. *Priye chāruseelé*

Beloved! Whose behaviour is so beautiful! Give up this baseless pride!
Cupid's fire is burning me now. Give my mind the pleasure of drinking the honey of your lotus face!
If you say something, the moonlight of your sparkling teeth will dispel the terrible darkness of fear!
Let the moon of your face prompt the chakora (nightbird) which is my eyes to drink the nectar of your quivering lower lip!

If you are really angry with me, show your anger by inflicting wounds on me with the arrows of your sharp nails!
Imprison me with your arms! Bite me with your teeth!
Do whatever will give you pleasure!

You are my adornment! You are my life!
You are the gem from the sea of Samsara!
"You be always attached to me", this is my heart's endeavour!

O! Creeperlike One! (Frail One!)
Your eyes, even though are like blue lotuses,
also look like dark clouds!
If it pleases you, my dark form, through the fancy of
Cupid's arrows, fittingly corresponds (to them).

स्फुरतु कुचकुम्भयोरुपरि मणिमञ्जरी रञ्जयतु तव हृदयदेशम्

रसतु रशनापि तव घनजघनमण्डले घोषयतु मन्मथ निदेशम् (प्रिये)

Sphuratu kucakumbhayorupari maṇimanjarī ranjayatu tava hrudayadéham

Rasatu raśanāpi tava ghanajaghanamandalé ghoṣayatu manmatha nidésam (priyé)

स्थल कमलगञ्जनं मम हृदयरञ्जनं जनितरतिरङ्ग परभागम्

भण मसृणवाणि करवाणि पदपङ्कजं सरसलसदलक्तकरागम्॥ (प्रिये)

Sthala kamalaganjanam mama

hrudayaranjanam janitaratiranga parabhāgam

Bhaṇa masruṇavāni karavaṇi padapankajam sarasalasa-dalaktakarāgam (priyé)

स्मरगरलखण्डनं मम शिरसि मण्डनं देहि पदपल्लवमुदारम्

ज्वलति मयि दारुणो मदन कदनारुणो हरतु तदुपाहित विकारम्॥ (प्रिये)

Smaragaralakhanḍanam mama śirasi manḍanam déhi padapallavamudāram

Jwalati mayi dāruno madana kadanāruṇo haratu tadupāhita vikāram (priyé)

इति चटुलचाटुपटुचारु भुरवैरिणो राधिकामधि वचनजातम्

जयति पद्मावतीरमण जयदेव कवि भारती भणित मति शातम्॥ (प्रिये)

Iti caṭulacāṭu paṭucāru bhuravairino rādhikāmadhi vacanajātam

Jayati padmāvati ramana jayadeva kavi bhāratī bhaṇitamati śātam (priyé)

Let the string of pearls stir over your two round breasts
and please the region of your heart!
Let the girdle on your heavy hips shine
and proclaim the order of the god of love!

Your lotus feet, outshine the red hibiscus flower,
evoke joy in my heart, and generate another facet
in the scene of loveplay!
Speak! Softspoken One!
May I colour them red with the vegetable dye?

Adorn my head with your soft feet, tender like fresh sprouts
and destroy the poison injected by the god of love!
The torment of Love, burns in me fiercely like the Sun,
Let (your feet) destroy the disorder created thereby.

Let these clever, coaxing, loving words spoken to Radha by Krishna, the Enemy of Mura,
and sung by the Sanskrit poet Jayadeva, husband of Padmavati,
be victorious!

राग : कल्याणि Rāga : Kalyāṇi

5. सखि हे केशिमथनमुदारम्
रमय मया सह मदनमनोरथ भावितया सविकारम् ॥
Sakhi hé késimathanamudāram
Ramaya mayā saha madanamanoratha bhāvitayā savikāram

निभृत निकुञ्जगृहं गतया निशि रहसि निलीय वसन्तम्
चकित विलोकित सकल दिशारति रभसरसेन हसन्तम् ॥ (सखि)
Nibhruta nikunja gruham gatayā niśi rahasi nilīya vasantam
Cakita vilokita sakala diśāratirabhasaraséna hasantam
(Sakhi)

प्रथम समागम लज्जितया पटुचाटुशतैरनुकूलम
मृदुमधुरस्मित भाषितया शिथिलीकृतज धनदुकूलम् ॥ (सखि)
Prathama samāgama lajjitayā patucātuśatairanukūlam
Mrudumadhura smita bhāṣitayā śithilīkrutaja dhana dukūlam
(Sakhi)

किसलय शयन निवेशितया चिरमुरसि ममैव शयानम्
कृत परिरम्भण चुम्बनया परिरम्य कृताधरपानम् ॥ (सखि)
Kisalaya śayananivéśitayā ciramurasi mamaiva śayānam
Kruta parirambhaṇa cumbanayā pariramya krutādharapānam
(Sakhi)

अलसनिमीलित लोचनया पुलकावलि ललित कपोलम्
श्रमजल सकल कलेवरया वरमदन मदादति लोलम् ॥ (सखि)
Alasanimīlita locanayā pulakāvali lalita kapolam
Śramajala sakala kalévarayā varamadana madādati lolam
(Sakhi)

5. *Sakhi hé kéśimathanamudāram*

O! Friend! Make Krishna, the benevolent Destroyer of Kesi! sport with me, who am tormented with imagining the fulfilment of Love!

I imagine:
I go at night in secret to the lonely forest dwelling,
where he lies, and suddenly see him, laughing in a mood of lovemaking!

At the first encounter, I am shy and he coaxes me with hundreds of flatteries;
I speak through a soft, sweet smile and he
removes the silken robe on my hip!

I lie on the bed of creepers, and for long
he too lies on my bosom,
I embrace him, kiss him, he clasps me and kisses my lips.

My eyes languish and close, with the thrill of touch of
his cheeks on my body, whole of which gets wet with sweat,
He shakes with the intoxication of love.

कोकिल कलरव कूजितया जितमनसिज तन्त्र विचारम्
श्लथ कुसुमाकुला कुन्तलया नखलिखित घनस्तनभारम्॥ (सखि)
Kokila kalarava kūjitayā jitamanasija tantra vicāram
Ślatha kusumākulā kuntalayā nakhalikhita ghanastana bhāram (Sakhi)

चरण रणितमणि नूपुरया परिपूरित सुरत वितानम्
मुखर विश्रङ्खल मेखलया सकचग्रह चुमबनदानम् (सखि)
Caraṇa raṇitamaṇi nūpuraya paripūrita surata vitānam
Mukhara viśrunkhala mékhalayā sakacagraha cumbanadānam (Sakhi)

रतिसुख समय रसालसया दरमुकुलित नयनसरोजम्
निःसह निपतित तनुलतया मधुसूदन मुदित मनोजम्॥ (सखि)
Ratisukha samaya rasālasayā daramukulita nayana sarojam
Nissaha nipatita tanulatayā Madhusūdana mudita manojam (Sakhi)

श्री जयदेव भणितमिदमतिशय मधुरिपु निधुवन शीलम्
सुख मुत्कण्ठित गोप वधू कथितं वितनोतु सलीलम्॥ (सखि)
Śrī Jayadéva bhanitamidamatiśaya Madhuripu nidhuvana śīlam
Sukha mutkanṭhita gopa vadhū kathitam vitanotu saḷīlam (Sakhi)

I coo like a cuckoo, and he knows that he has mastered
the secret of winning my heart over
My hair is full of faded flowers
and I bear the burden of my heavy breasts, marked by his nails!

My anklets jingle on my feet, as he completes the rite of love,
the freed girdle falls resonantly, as he holds the hair and gives
a kiss!

I languish as a result of the good time I had of lovemaking,
His lotus eyes are barely open!
Helplessly I fall like a creeper, Krishna, the Killer of demon
Madhu, is happy with my love.

Let this song sung by Sri Jayadeva, about the fantasy of Radha
making love to Krishna, the Enemy of Madhu,
told to the cowherdess listening eagerly and with joy,
bestow happiness.

राग : वसन्त Rāga : Vasanta

6. विरहति हरिरिह सरसवसन्ते
नृत्यति युवति जनेन समं सखि विरहिजनस्य दुरन्ते॥
Virahati Haririha sarasavasanté
Nrutyati yuvati janéna samam sakhi virahijanasya duranté

ललितलवंगलता परिशीलन कोमल मलय समीरे
मधुकर निकर करम्बित कोकिल कूजित कुञ्जकुटीरे (विरहति)
Lalitalavangalatā pariśīlana komala malaya samīré
Madhukara nikara karambita kokila kūjita kunjakuṭīré
(Virahati)

उन्मदमदन मनोरथपथिक वधूजन जनित विलापे
अलिकुल संकुल कुसुम समूह निराकुल वकुल कलापे (विरहति)
Unmada madana manoratha pathika vadhūjana janita vilāpé
Alikula sankula kusuma samūha nirākula vakula kalāpé
(Virahati)

मदन महीपति कनक दण्डरुचि केशर कुसुमविकासे
मिलित शिलीमुख पाटलिपटल कृत स्मर तूण विलासे (विरहति)
Madana mahīpati kanaka dandaruci késara kusuma vikāsé
Milita śilīmukha pāṭalipaṭala kruta smara tūṇa vilāsé
(Virahati)

विगलित लज्जित जगदवलोकन तरुण करुण कृतहासे
विरहि निकृन्तन कुन्तमुखा कृति केतक दन्तुरिताशे (विरहति)
Vigalita lajjita jagadavalokana taruṇa karuṇa krutahāsé
virahi nikruntana kunta mukhā kruti ketaka danturitāśé
(Virahati)

6. *Virahati Haririha*

In pleasant springtime, Krishna wanders here
and dances with young girls, Friend!
to the dismay of separated lovers!

When soft southern breeze blows and kisses the tender clove creepers,
and forest dwellings reverberate with the humming of bees
and the cooing of cuckoos (Krishna wanders...)

When the brides of travellers cry out in insane love fantasies
and the bees gather around clusters of flowers on tree branches,
(Krishna wanders...)

When the fragrance of deer musk permeates the fresh leaves of the Tamala trees,
and the petals of Kimsuka clusters break the hearts of youngsters (Krishna wanders...)

Saffron flowers bloom, like the golden sceptres of the King of love and Trumpet flowers with bees on them look like arrows in Cupid's quiver!

मृगमदसौरभ रभस वंश वदन वदल मालतमाले
युव जन हृदय विदारण मनसि जन स्वरुचि किंशुकजाले (विरहति)
Mrugamada saurabha rabhasa vamśa vadan vadala mālatamālé
Yuva jana hrudaya vidāraṇa manasi jana swaruci kimśukajālé
(Virahati)

माधविका परिमल ललिते नव मालिक जाति सुगन्धौ
मुनि मनसामपि मोहन कारिणि तरुण कारण बन्धौ (विरहति)
Mādhavikā parimala lalité nava mālika jāti sugandhau
Muni manasāmapi mohana kāriṇi taruṇa kāraṇa bandhau
(Virahati)

स्फुरदति मुक्तलता परिरम्भण मुकुलित पुलकित चूते
वृन्दावन विपिने परिसर परिगत यमुना जलपूते (विरहति)
Sphuradati muktalatā parirambhaṇa mukulita pulakita cūté
Vrundāvana vipiné parisara parigata Yamunā jalapūté
(Virahati)

श्री जयदेव भणितमिदमुदयति हरिचरण स्मृति सारम्
सरस वसन्त समय वनवर्णनमनुगत मदन विकारम् (विरहति)
Śrī Jayadéva bhaṇitamidamudayati haricaraṇa smruti sāram
Sarasa Vasanta samaya vana varṇana manugata madana vikāram
(Virahati)

Seeing the entire world give up modesty, the buds bloom, as if in deriding laughter!,
and the thorny Ketaka flowers look like spikes to wound the hearts of separated lovers!

When the fragrance of clinging creepers mingle with the sweet smells of fresh jasmine garlands,
and the bonds of youth captivate even the hearts of sages!

Young mango trees thrill by the embrace of twining creepers,
and the Brindavan forest is washed by the wandering waters of the Yamuna river, (Krishna wanders...)

What has been said here by Sri Jayadeva
evokes the memory of Krishna's feet,
describing the forest conditions in pleasant springtime
creating a mood of love making.

राग : खरहरप्रिया

Rāga : Kharaharapriya

7. हरि हरि हतादरतया गता सा कुपितेव
मामियं वलिता विलोक्य वृतं वधूनिचयेन
सापराधतया मयापि न वारितातिभयेन (हरि हरि)

Hari hari hatādaratayā gatā sā kupitéva
Māmiyam valitā vilokya vrutam vadhūnicayéna
Sāparādhatayā mayāpi na vāritātibhayéna (Hari hari)

किं करिष्यति किं वदिष्यति सा चिरं विरहेण
किं धनेन जनेन किं मम जीवितेन गृहेण॥ (हरि हरि)

Kim kariṣyati kim vadiṣyati sā ciram virahéṇa
kim dhanéna janéna kim mama jīviténa gruhéṇa
(Hari hari)

चिन्तयामि तदाननं कुटिलभ्रु कोपभरेण
शोणपद्ममिवोपरि भ्रमनाकुलं भ्रमरेण॥ (हरि हरि)

Cintayāmi tadānanam kuṭilabhru kopabharéṇa
Śoṇapadmamivopari bhramanākulam bhramaréṇa
(Hari hari)

तामहं हृदि संगतामनिशं भृशं रमयामि
किं वनेऽनुसरामि तामिह किं वृथा विलपामि॥ (हरि हरि)

Tāmaham hrudi sangatāmaniśam bhruśam ramayāmi
Kim vané nusarāmi tāmiha kim vruthā vilapāmi
(Hari hari)

7. *Hari Hari hataadaratayā*

Alas! She has gone away in anger, due to my wayward ways!
Seeing me surrounded by the array of girls!
Feeling guilty and afraid, I did not stop her!

What will she do? What will she say?
due to this long separation?
What is the use of wealth, life, people and home?

I think of her face, her brows knit in anger,
as the red lotus flower over which hovers the bee.

In my heart, I shall ceaselessly try to please her, who has gone away!
Why do I follow her in the forest? Why do I weep for her here?

तन्वि खिन्नमसूयया हृदयं तवाकलयामि
तन्न वेद्मि कुतो गतासि न तेन तेऽनुनयामि ॥ (हरि हरि)
Tanvi khinnamasūyayā hrudayam tavākalayāmi
Tanna vedmi kuto gatāsi na téna té nunayāmi (Hari hari)

दृश्यसे पुरतो गतागतमेव मे विदधासि
किं पुरेव ससंभ्रमं परिरम्भणं न ददासि ॥ (हरि हरि)
Druśyasé purato gatāgataméva mé vidadhāsi
Kim puréva sasambhramam parirambhaṇam na dadāsi
(Hari hari)

क्षम्यतामपरं कदापि तवेदृशं न करोमि
देहि सुन्दरि दर्शनं मम मन्मथेन दुनोमि (हरि हरि)
Kṣamyatāmaparam kadāpi tavédruśam na karomi
Dehi sundari darśanam mama manmathéna dunomi
(Hari hari)

वर्णितं जयदेवकेन हरेरिदं प्रवणेन
किन्दु बिल्वसमुद्र सम्भव रोहिणी रमणेन ॥ (हरि हरि)
Varṇitam Jayadevakéna haréridam pravaṇéna
Kindu bilwasamudra sambhava rohiṇī ramaṇéna
(Hari hari)

O! Frail One! I know that your heart is broken by jealousy
But I do not know where you have gone! How can I follow you?

You seem to appear and disappear in my fancy
Why don't you give me the tremulous embraces like before?

Please forgive me! hereafter, I won't do this to you!
O! Beautiful One! Let me see you. I am being burnt by Cupid.

Krishna's condition is described thus with devotion, by Jayadeva, who comes from the village Kindubilwa, like the moon from the sea.

राग : भैरवि

Rāga : Bhairavi

8. हरि हरि याहि माधव याहि केशव मा वद कैतववादं
तामनुसर सरसीरुहलोचन या तव हरति विषादं ॥
रजनि जनित गुरुजागर रागकषायितमलस निवेशम्
वहति नयन मनुरागमिव स्फुटमुदित रसाभिनिवेशम् ॥ (हरि हरि)

Hari hari yāhi Mādhava yāhi Kéśava mā vada kaitavavādam
Tāmanusara sarasīruhalocana yā tava harati viṣādam
Rajani janita guru jāgara rāgakaṣāyitamalasanivéśam
Vahati nayana manurāgamiva sphuṭamudita rasābhinivéśam
(Hari hari)

कज्जलमलिन विलोचन चुम्बन विरचित नीलमरूपम्
दशन वसनमरुणं तव कृष्ण तनोति तनोरनुरूपम् ॥ (हरि हरि)

Kajjalamalina vilocana cumbana viracita nīlamarūpam
Daśana vasanamaruṇam tava kruṣṇa tanoti tanoranurūpam
(Hari hari)

वपुरनुहरति तव स्मरसङ्गरखरनख रक्षतरेखम्
मरकत शकल कलित कल धौत लिपेरिव रति जयलेखम् (हरि हरि)

Vapuranuharati tava smarasangarakharanakha rakṣatarékham
Marakata śakala kalita kala dhauta lipériva rati jayalékham
(Hari hari)

8. *Hari! Hari yaahi Mādhava*

O! Madhava! O! Kesava!
You Krishna! Don't tell me your false alibis!
Go after her, O! Lotuseyed One! she will dispel your sorrow!
Due to lying lazy, after spending the night awake making love,
Your eyes convey the delight of awakened love!

Due to kissing her eyes darkened with collyrium, Your lips normally red, have assumed a black hue, in consonance with your body's colour!

Your body, wounded by nails in the battle of love, resembles the emerald stone, etched in golden letters, a written evidence, as it were, of the triumph of loveplay!

चरणकमल गलदलक्तक सिक्रमिदं तव हृदयमुदारम्
दर्शयतीव बर्हिमदन द्रमुनव किसलय परिवारम्॥ (हरि हरि)

Caraṇa kamala galadalaktaka sikramidam
tava hrudayamudāram
Darśayatīva barhimadana drumanava kisalaya parivāram
(Hari hari)

दशन पदं भवदधरगतं मम जनयति चेतसि खेदम्
कथयति कथमधुनापि मया सह तव वपुरेतदभेदम्॥ (हरि हरि)

Daśana padam bhavadadharagatam mama janayati cétasi khédam
Kathayati kathamadhunāpi maya saha tava vapurétadabhédam
(Hari hari)

वहिरिव मलिन तरं तव कृष्ण मनोऽपि भविष्यति नूनं
कथमथ वञ्चयसे जनमनुगतमसम शर ज्वर दूनं (हरि हरि)

Vahiriva malina taram tava kṛṣṇa manopi bhaviṣyati nūnam
Kathamatha vancayasé janamanugatamasama śara jwara dūnam (Hari hari)

भ्रमति भवानबलाकवलाय वनेषु किमत्र विचित्रम्
प्रथयति पूतनिकैव वधूवधनिर्दय बाल चरित्रम्॥ (हरि हरि)

Bhramati bhawānabalā kavalāya vanéṣu kimatra vicitram
Prathayati pūtanikaiva vadhū vadha nirdaya bāla caritram
(Hari hari)

श्री जयदेव भणित रति वञ्चित खण्डित युवति विलापम्।
शृणुत सुधामधुरं विबुधा विबुधालयतोऽपि दुरापम्॥ (हरि हरि)

Śrī Jayadéva bhaṇita rati vancita khandita yuvati vilāpam
Śruṇuta sudhā madhuram vibudhā vibudhālayato pi durāpam
(Hari hari)

Your benevolent bosom has been wetted by the drops of vegetable dye from her lotus feet;
these display, as it were, clusters of buds from the tree of Cupid!

The teeth mark on your lower lip creates sorrow in my heart!
It tell me even now that I am inseparable from your body!

O! Krishna! Darkhued One! Your outside is no doubt black but blacker definitely is your mind
Otherwise, how do you deceive a person who ever follows you, fevered by the arrows of Cupid?

What is surprising in this: that you wander in the woods to kill helpless women!
Pootana's fate proclaims your cruel childhood history of killing women!

The wail of a young woman deceived in love (by Krishna) has been described by Sri Jayadeva!
Listen, learned men! to this sweet nectar,
difficult to get even from heaven!

राग : पूर्वकल्याणी Rāga : Poorvakalyani

9. माधवे मा कुरु मानिनि मानमये
हरिरभिसरति वहति मधु पवने
किमपरमधिक सुखं सखि भुवने (माधवे)
Mādhavé mā kuru mānini mānamayé
Harirabhisarati vahati madhu pawané
Kimaparamadhika sukham sakhi bhuvané (Mādhavé)

ताल फलादपि गुरुमतिसरसम्
किं विफलीकुरुषे कुचकलशम्॥ (माधवे)
Tālaphalādapi gurumati sarasam
Kim viphalikuruṣé kucakalaśam (Mādhavé)

कति न कथित मिदमनुपदमचिरम्।
मा परिहर हरिमतिशय रुचिरम्॥ (माधवे)
Kati na kathita midamanupadamaciram
Mā parihara hari matiśaya ruciram (Mādhavé)

किमिति विषीदसि रोदिषि विकला
विहसति युवति सभा तव सकला॥ (माधवे)
Kimiti viṣīdasi rodiṣi vikalā
Vihasati yuvati sabhā tava sakalā (Mādhavé)

9. *Maadhavé mā kuru*

O! Proud One! Don't show your pride towards Madhava!
he is full of pride too!

Krishna comes to sport, when the sweet winds blow
Friend! what is a greater joy in this world?

Your heavy potlike breasts are tastier than palmfruits
Why waste them?

How many times have I told you:
Don't resist Krishna, who can entertain so wonderfully!

Why do you feel sad and desolate and cry?
All your young girlfriends are laughing at you!

सजल नलिनीदल शीतल शयने
हरिमवलोकय सफलय नयने ॥ (माधवे)
Sajala nalinīdala śītala śayané
Harimavalokaya saphalaya nayané (Mādhavé)

जनयसि मनसि किमिति गुरुखेदम्
शृणु मम वचनम नीहित भेदम् ॥ (माधवे)
Janayasi manasi kimiti gurukhédam
Śruṇu mama vacanamanīhita bhédam (Mādhavé)

हरिरूपयातु वदतु बहुमधुरम्
किमिति करोषि हृदयमति विधुरम् ॥ (माधवे)
Harirūpayātu vadatu bahumadhuram
Kimiti karoṣi hrudayamati vidhuram (Mādhavé)

श्री जयदेव भणित मतिललितम्
सुखयतु रसिकजनं हरिचरितम् ॥ (माधवे)
Śrī Jayadéva bhaṇita matilalitam
Sukhayatu rasikajanam Haricaritam (Mādhavé)

Feast your eyes, looking at Krishna
lying on the cool bed of wet lotuses!

Why generate this heavy regret in your heart?
Listen to my words about his regret in changing his heart.

Let Krishna come and speak sweet words!
Why do you make your heart impregnable?

Let this playful song of Sri Jayadeva
about Krishna's legends, please connoisseurs!

राग : नाटभैरवि Rāga : Nātabhairavi

10. यामि हे कमिह शरणं सखीजन वचनवञ्चिता
कथित समयेऽपि हरिरहह न ययौ वनम्
मम विफल मिदममलरूपमपि यौवनम् ॥ (यामि)
Yāmi hé kamiha śaraṇam sakhījana vacanavancitā
Kathita samayépi harirahaha na yayau vanam
Mama viphala midamamala rūpamapi yauvanam (Yāmi)

यदनुगमनाय निशि गहनमपि शीलितम्
तेन मम हृदयमिदमसमशरकीलितम् ॥ (यामि)
Yadanugamanāya niśi gahanamapi śīlitam
Tena mama hrudayamidamasamaśarakīlitam (Yāmi)

मम मरणमेव वरमतिवितथकेतना
किमिह विषहामि विरहानलमचेतना ॥ (यामि)
Mama maraṇaméva varamativitatha kétanā
Kimiha viṣahāmi virahānalamacétanā (Yāmi)

मामहह विधुरयति मधुर मधुयामिनी
कापि हरिमनुभवति कृतसुकृतकामिनी ॥ (यामि)
Māmahaha vidhurayati madhura madhuyāminī
Kāpi harimanubhavati krutasukruta kāminī (Yāmi)

10. *Yaami Hé*

In whom can I seek refuge? I have been duped by friend's words!

Alas! at the appointed time, Krishna did not come to the woods!

The flawless form of my youth is wasted now.

He, to reach whom, I went at night to the dense forest has pierced my heart with the arrows of love!

My death is better than living in this useless body
Why should I suffer the burning fire of separation?

Alas! The sweet spring night tortures me
Some girl, who has done punya, is enjoying Krishna now!

अहह कलयामि वल्यादिमणिभूषणम्
हरि विरह दहन वहनेन बहुदूषणम् ॥ (यामि)
Ahaha kalayāmi valyādimaṇibhūṣaṇam
Hari viraha dahana vahanéna bahudūṣaṇam (Yāmi)

कुसुम सुकुमार तनुमतनु शर लीलया
स्त्रगपि हृदि हन्ति मामतिविषमशीलया ॥ (यामि)
Kusuma sukumāra tanumatanu śara līlayā
Sragapi hrudi hanti māmativiṣamaśīlayā (Yāmi)

अहमिह निवसामि नगणित वन वेतसा
स्मरति मधुसूदनो मामपि न चेतसा ॥ (यामि)
Ahamiha nivasāmi nagaṇitavanavétasā
Smarati madhusūdano māmapi na cétasā (Yāmi)

हरिचरण शरण जयदेव कवि भारती
वसतु हृदि युवतिरिव कोमल कलावती ॥ (यामि)
Hari caraṇa śaraṇa Jayadéva kavi bhāratī
Vasatu hrudi yuvatiriva komala kalāvatī (Yāmi)

Alas! All the jewelled bangles and ornaments I wear,
I feel, are a disgrace, due to the pain of separation from Krishna!

My body, fragile like a flower, due to the arrows of Cupid, is hurt even by a garland, in my present difficult state!

Here do I live among myriad forest reeds
Krishna, Killer of Madhu does not
remember me in his heart!

Let the poetry of poet Jayadeva rest at the feet of Hari like a young girl, skilled in fine arts!

# SONGS OF VIDYAPATI

*(14th-15th Century A.D.)*

| | *Song* | *Rāga* |
|---|---|---|
| 1. | Madhav bahut minati karon toy | Dhanasree |
| 2. | Nandak nandan kadambak tarutar | Gauri |
| 3. | Sakhi he katahu na dekhiya Madhai | Kapi |
| 4. | Madhav hamar ratal door des | Behag |
| 5. | Nahaye utali teere rai Kamalamukhi | Todi |
| 6. | Kunj bhavan sanye nikasali re | Sarang |
| 7. | He Hari He Hari sunia sravan bhari | Bilawal |
| 8. | Virah vyakul bakul taru tar | Desh |
| 9. | Hari sam anan Hari sam lochan | Lalit |
| 10. | Madhav dekhali viyogini bame | Asaveri |

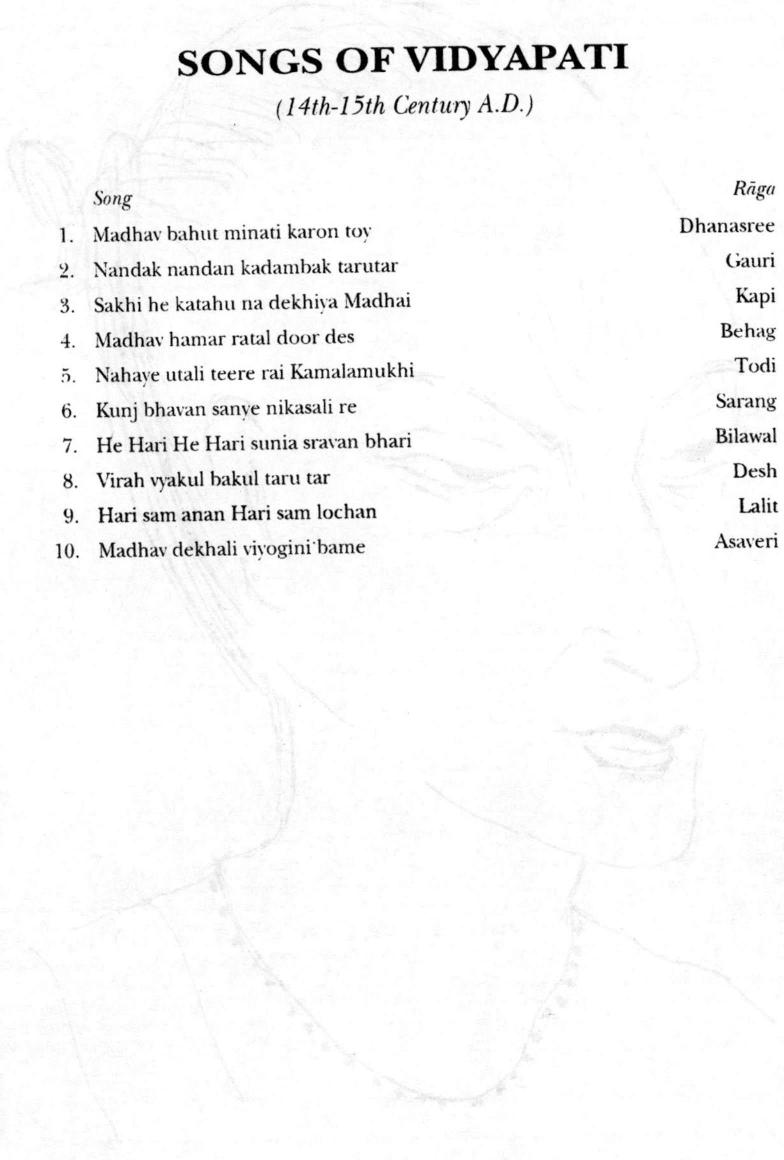

*VIDYAPATI*

# VIDYAPATI (1350-1460)

Vidyapati, the court poet of Mithila, during the reign of Raja Shivasimha was born in Bisapi, a village in Mithila. He received his education from Harimishra, a reputed scholar. Vidyapati's poetic genius attracted everyone, including the ruler Shivasimha and his queen Lakhima Devi.

Vidyapati was a contemporary of Chandidas, the Bengali poet whose approach to religion and poetry was similar to that of Vidyapati.

Vidyapati's songs are full of erotic imagery, like Jayadeva's but also soaked in devotion and melodious grace.

Vidyapati wrote his first poem when he was hardly 20 years old. His major work is: *Padāvali,* a collection of hundreds of his poems, covering his entire life period.

His poetic obsession was the love of Radha and Krishna, the Divine couple and he has dealt with it with elegance, simplicity, sentiment and sensuousness. The eager longing to meet, the bliss of union and the sadness of separation of the lovers are all dealt with passion and sincerity.

The songs of Vidyapati are even now sung daily by the women of Mithila.

राग : धनाश्री Rāga : Dhanasree

1. माधव, बहुत मिनति कर तोहि। दए तुलसी तिल देह समरपल
दया जनि छाड़न मोहि। गनइत दोस गुन-लेस न पाओन
जन तोहें करन विचार। तोहें जगत जगनाथ कहाओसि जग बहार नहि छार॥
किअ मानुस पसु पखि भये जनमिअ। अथवा कीट पतंग।
करम विपाक गतागत पुनु पुनु। मति रह तुअ परसग॥
भनइ विद्यापति अतिसय कातर तरइते ई भव-सिन्धु।
तुअ पद-पल्लव केर अवलम्बन तिला एक देह दिनबन्धु॥

Mādhav, bahut minati kar tohi dayé tulsi til déh samarpal
Dayā jani chādan mohil | Ganait dos gun-lés na pāon
Jan tohéṅ karan vicar | tohéṅ jagat Jaganāth kahaosī
Jag bahār nahi chār ||
Kia mānus pasu pakṣi bhayé janamia | athavā kīt patang |
Karam vipāk gatāgat punu punu | mati rah tua parasag ||
Bhanayi Vidyāpati atisay kātar tarayité ī bhav-sindhu |
Tua pad-pallav kér avalamban tilā yék déh dinabandhu ||

1. O! Madhava! Lord of Lakshmi!
I beseech you very much
Show me a little mercy.
When I think of you,
I do not get anything bad, only good,
O! Lord of Universe! Yours is the universe
Life becomes a festival of spring, not hell.
According to my karma, again and again
I may assume the form of a man, animal, bird
or insect or reptile.
But let my mind rest on You!
Says Vidyapati: You are the miraculous means
to cross the ocean of Samsara!
Your lotus feet are the only refuge
O! Friend of the poor and afflicted!

राग : गौरी Rāga : Gauri

2. बन्दक बन्दक कदम्बक तरु-तरु धिरे-धिरे मुरलि बजाव।
समय सँकेत-निकेतन बइसल बेरि-बेरि बोलि पठाव॥
सामरि, तोहरा लागि अनुखन विकल मुरारि॥
जमुनाक तिर उपवन उद्वेगल फिरि-फिरि ततहि निहारि।
गोरस बेचए अबइत जाइत जनि-जनि पुछ बनमारि॥
तोंहे मतिमान, सुमति मधुसूदन वचन सुनह किछु मोरा।
भनइ विद्यापति सुन बरजौवति बन्दह मन्द-किसोरा॥

Bandak nandan kadambak taru-taru dhiré-dhiré murali bajāv ।
Samay sankét-nikétan bayisal béri-béri boli paṭhāv ।।
Sāmari, toharā lāgi anukhan vikal Murari ।
Jamunāk tir upvan udvégal phiri-phiri tat-hi nihāri ।
Goras bécayé ab-it jāyit jani-jani puch Banmari ।।
Tohé matimān, sumati Madhusūdan vacan sunah kichu morā ।
Bhanayi vidyāpati sun barjauvati bandah nand-kisorā ।।

2. Sree Krishna, Nanda's son, is slowly playing the flute,
under the Kadamba tree.
Sitting at the meeting place (knowing the time for the meet)
He is calling again and again.
O! Beautiful One! for your sake,
Every moment, Krishna, Mura's Enemy, is suffering.
On the banks of the Yamuna river, in the gardens,
Krishna is looking again and again at the path
(by which you come)
Krishna, Vanamali, is asking every person,
who comes to sell milk and curds, about you.
Hence, O! Wise One! please listen to a few words
of mine about the goodminded Krishna, the Killer of the demon, Madhu.
Says Vidyapati, O! venerable Young Girl!
Worship, Krishna, the son of Nanda!

राग : कापि Rāga : Kapi

3. सखि हे कतहु न देखिअ मधाई
काँप शरीर धीर नहिं मानस
अबधि नियर भेलि आई।

Sakhi hé katahu na dékhia Madhāee
Kāmp śarīr dhīr nahim mānas
Abadhi niyar bhéli āyi

माधब मास तिथि भंड़ माधब
अबधि कइए पिआ गेला।
कुच-जुग संभु परसि कर बोललन्हि
तें परतिति मोहि भेला।

Mādhab mās tithi bhanḍ Mādhab
Abadhi kaié piya gélā
Kuchajug sambhu parasi kar bolalanhi
Tén paratiti mohi bhélā

मृगमद चानन परिमल कुंकुम
के बोल सीतल चन्दा
पिअ बिसलेख अनल जओं बरिसए
बिपति चिन्हिअ भल मन्दा।

Mrugamad chānan parimal kumkuma
Ké ból sītal chandā
Pia bisalékh anal jaon barisaé
Bipati chinhaa bhal mandā

भनई विद्यापति सुन बर जौबति
चित जनु झाँखह आजे
पिअ बिसलेख-क्लेस मेटाएत
बालँभ बिलसि समाजे।

Bhanaī Vidyāpati sun bar jaubati
Chit janu jhānkhaha ājé
Piya visalékhaklésa metāyét
Bālanbh bilasi samājé

3. O! Friend! For how long have I not seen Madhav!
My body is trembling, my mind is unsteady,
the day of meeting is nearing.

Ekadasi day of Vaisakh month,
which is the meeting day with the beloved has gone!
The opportunity to enjoy sweet words from him, while he
fondles my breasts with his hands, is lost.

Kasturi, sandal paste, perfumed kumkum
not to speak of the cool moon
all these have become like burning fire
due to separation from the beloved.

Says Vidyapati: Listen good girl!
Today don't feel upset in your mind.
To dispel the sorrow of separation
the boy Krishna flourishes in the community.

राग : बेहाग

Rāga : Behag

4. माधव हमर रटल दूर देस
केओ न कहए सखि कुसल-सनेस।
Mādhav hamar ratal door dés
Kéo na kahayé sakhi kusala sanés

जुग-जुग जिबथु बसथु लाख कोस
हमर अभाग हनक नहि दोस।
Jug-jug jibathu basathu lākh kós
Hamar abhāg hanak nahi dós

हमरे करमे भेल बिहि बिपरीत
तेजल माधव पुरुब पिरीत।
Hamaré karamé bhél bihi bipareet
Téjal Mādhav purub pireet

हृदयक बेदन बान समान
आनक दुःख आन नहि जान
Hridayak bédan bān samān
Ānak dukh ān nahi jān

भनई विद्यापति कवि जयराम
दैब लिखल परिनत फल बाम॥
Bhanai Vidyāpati kavi jayarām
Daib likhal parinat phal bām

4. Our Madhava has gone away to a far off place
No one has brought any message about his wellbeing, O! friend!

We may live for many ages, reside in a myriad bodies
(without seeing him). This is our misfortune; no fault of His!

Brahma, the Creator has made our Karma awry
that is why our beloved Madhava has left us.

My heart's pain is skyhigh,
I do not know of others' sorrow.

Says poet Vidyapati,
the net result of Godwritten destiny is awry.

राग : तोडी Rāga : Todi

5. नहाए उठलि तीरे राइ कमलमुखि समुख हेरल वर कान
Nahāyé uthali teeré rāyee kamalamukhi samukh heral var kaan

गुरुजनसंग लाज धनि नत-मुखि कईसन हेरब बयान
Gurujanasang lāj dhani natamukhi kaisan hérab bayān

सखि हे, अपरुब चातुरि गोरि सब जन तेजि कए अगुसरि संचरु आड़ वदन तँह मोड़ि
Sakhi Hé, aparub chāturi gori sab jan téji kayé agusari sancharu āḍ vadan tanh modi

तहाँ पुन मोति-हार तोरि फेंकल कहइत हार टुटि गेल।
Tahān puna moti-hār tori fénkal kahait hār tuti gél

सब जन एक-एक चुनि संचरु स्याम-दरस धनि लेल
Sab jan ék-ék chuni sancharu syām daras dhani lél

नयन-चकोर कान्ह मुख ससि-वर कएल अमिय-रस-पान।
Nayana chakor kānh mukh sasi-var kaél amiya ras pān

दुहु दुहु, दरसन रसहु पसारब कवि विद्यापति भान।
Duhu duhu darsan rasahu pasārab kavi Vidyapati bhān

5. Lotusfaced Radha got up on the riverbank, after her bath and saw handsome Krishna.

In the company of others, modesty made her lower her face
and think: how to send a message (to Krishna)

O! maid!, the fair one was wonderfully clever!
All persons hastened ahead to see Krishna and hid his face.

Then she threw her pearl necklace, shouting
my necklace is broken!

Everyone went in search of the pearls,
And she had a good look at Krishna

Her eyes drank the beauty of Krishna, like nectar
as the Chakora bird drinks the rays of the moon.

The sight of Krishna was long and enjoyable
Says poet Vidyapati.

राग : सारंग

Rāga : Sarang

6. कुंज-भवन सएँ निकसलि रे रोकल गिरिधारी
Kunj bhavan sayé nikasali ré rokala Giridhāri

एकहि नगर बसु माधव हे जनि कुरु बटमारी।
Ékahi nagar basu Mādhava Hé jani karu baṭamārī

छाड़ु कान्ह मोर आँचर रे फाटत नव-सारी।
Cchādu kanha mor ānchar Ré fātata nava sāree

अपजस होएत जगत भरि हे जनि करिअ उधारी।
Apajasa hoét jagat bhari Hé jani karia udhārī

संगक सखि अगुआइलि रे हम एकसरि नारी।
Sangak sakhi aguāili Ré Hum éksari nārī

दामिनी आए तुलाएलि एक राति अँधारी।
Dāminī āyé tulāyéli ék rāti andhārī

भनहि विद्यापति गाओल रे सुनु गुनमति नारी।
Bhanahi Vidyāpati gāol Ré sunu gunamati nārī

हरिक संग किछु डर नहि तोंहे परम गमारी।
Harik sang kītchu ḍar nahi tonhé param gamārī

6. When I came out of the garden,
Krishna, Giridhari, the one who held the mountain,
stopped me.

"O! Madhava!" (I said), "Don't we reside in the same city?
Please don't waylay me."

"Please leave, Krishna!, the end of my saree!
My new saree is tearing."

"I will be disgraced, the world over,
Don't make me naked!"

"My companions have gone ahead.
I, a woman, am alone!"

"Lightning is threatening to strike
The night is dark!"

Says Vidyapati, singing:
"Listen, good lady!
In Krishna's company, there is no fear!
You are a great fool!"

राग : बिलावल

Rāga : Bilawal

7. हे हरि हे हरि सुनिअ स्रवन भरि
अब न बिलासक बेरा।
गगन नखत छल से अबेकत भेल
कोकिल कुल कर फेरा।
चकबा मोर सोर कए चुप भेल
उठिअ मलिन भेल चंदा।
नगरक धेनु डगर कए संचर
कुमुदनि बस मकरंदा।
मुख केर पान सेहो रे मलिन भेल
अवसर भल नहि मंदा।
विद्यापति मन एहो न उचित थिक
जग भरि होएल निंदा॥

Hé Hari hé Hari sunia sravan bhari
Ab na bilāsak bérā ।
Gagan nakhat chal sé abekat bhél
Kokil kul kar phérā ।
Cakbā mor sor kayé cup bhél
Uṭhiya malin bhél candā ।
Nagarak dhénu dagar kayé sancar
Kumudani bas makarandā ।
Mukh kér pān sého ré malin bhél
Avsar bhal nahi mandā ।
Vidyāpati man yého na ucit thik
Jag bhari hoyél nindā ।।

7. O! Hari! O! Hari! Destroyer of sorrow!
Listen carefully!

This is not the time for play.

The stars in the sky have disappeared.

The koels are roaming here and there.

The peacocks have folded their feathers and become silent.

The moon has risen in the clouded sky,

The citizens are taking the cows home on the road;

The bees have settled inside the flowers.

Even to see the face, the time is not good;

Vidyapati says, this is not the right time,

The whole world will criticize.

राग : देश

Rāga : Desh

8. विरह व्याकुल बकुल तरुतर पेखल नन्द-कुमार रे।
नील नीरज नयन सएं सखि दरए नीर अपारे रे।
पेखि मलयज-पंक मृगमद तामरस घनसार रे।
निज पानि पल्लव मूँदि लोचन धरनि पड़ु असंभार रे।
बहए मन्द सुगन्धि सीतल मन्द मलय-समीर रे।
जनि प्रलय कालक प्रबल पाबक दहए सून सरीर रे॥
अधिक बेपथु टूटि पड़ खिति मसृन मुकुता-माल रे।
अनिल तरल तमाल तरुवर मुंच सुमनस जाल रे॥
मान-मनि तजि सुदति चलु जहि राय रसिक सुजान रे।
स्रुति सुखद अति सरस दण्डक कवि विद्यापति भान रे।

Virah vyākul bakul tarutar pékhal nand-kumār ré
Nīl nīraj nayan sayén sakhi darayé nīr apāré ré
Pékhi malayajā-pank mrugamad tāmaras ghansār ré
Nij pāni pallav mūndilocan dharani padu asambhār ré
Bahayé mand sugandhi sītal mand malay-sameera ré
Jani pralay kālak prabal pāvak dahayé sūn sarīr ré
Adhik vepathu ṭūṭi paḍ khiti masrun mukuta-māl ré
Anil taral tamāl taruvar munch sumanas jāl ré
Mān-ṃani taji sudati calu jahi rāi rasik sujān ré
Sruti sukhad ati saras dandak kavi vidyapati bhān ré

8. O! Son of Nanda! The sorrow of separation has grown like a tree in the mind.
O! Beloved, whose eyes are like the blue lotus
The waters beyond are fearful.
The sandal paste, lotus, Kasturi and camphor,
My own hand and tearfilled eyes
have become unbearable.
The slow, fragrant, cool Southern breeze,
(Malayamaruta)
is burning my empty body like the powerful fire
which rages at the time of deluge.
The oily pearlnecklace (on my body)
is like the earth broken up by a great quake,
The flowers are falling from my garland
as from a tree shaken by the wind.
I am like the beautiful girl, given up
by the clever, pleasure loving King.
This beautiful piece, so nice to hear
has been recited by the poet Vidyapati.

राग : ललित

Rāga : Lalit

9. हरि सम आनन हरि सम लोचन हरि तहां हरि बर आगी।
हरिहि चाहि हरि हरि न सोहाबए हरि हरि कए उठ जागी॥
Hari sama ānana hari sama locana hari tahāṅ hari bar āgī
Harihi cāhi hari hari na sohābayé hari hari kayé uṭh jāgī

माधव हरि रहु जल धर छाई
हरि नयनी धनि हरि-घरिनी जनि
हहि हेरइते दिन जाई॥
Mādhav hari rahu jal dhar chāyī
Hari nayanī dhani hari-gharinī jani
Hahi hérayité din jāyī

हरि भेल भार हार भेल हरि सम
हरि क बचब न सोहाबे।
हरिहि पइसि जे हरि जे नुकाएल
हरि चढि मोर बुझावे।
Hari bhél bhār hār ḅhél hari sam
Hari ka bacab na sohābé
Harihi payisi jé hari jé nukāyél
Hari caḍhi mor bujhāvé

हरिहि बचन पुनु हरि सए दरसन
सुकवि विद्यापति भाने।
राजा सिंवसिंह रूप नराएन
लखिमा देवि रमाने॥
Harihi bacan punu hari sayé darsan
Sukavi vidyāpati bhāne
Rājā sinvsimh rūp narāyén
Lakhimā dévi ramāné

9. The face is permeated by Hari
The eyes are full of Hari
Where there is Hari, there is benediction.
I only desire Hari, Only Hari is pleasing
I wake up saying: "Hari! Hari!"

Madhava, Hari, is hidden like the overcast cloud
Eyes are like the parched earth,
Waiting, waiting, days go by.

Meeting Hari can only be meeting Hari
Without Hari, I cannot sleep.
Like the rain waters, let
Hari quench my thirst.

The good poet Vidyapati sings again and again
of Hari's legends and meeting with Hari
to please Lakhima devi,
consort of King Shiv Singh Roop Narayan.

राग : असावेरि  Rāga : Asaveri

10. माधव देखलि बियोगिनि बामे अधर न हास बिलास सखी संग।
अहनिस जप तुअ नामे।
Mādhav dékhali viyogini bāmé adhar na hās bilās sakhī sang
Ahanis jap tua nāmé ।

आनन सरद सुधाकर सम तसु बोलए मधुर धुनि बानी।
कोमल अरुन कमल कुम्हिलाएल देखि मएँ अइलिहँ जानी।
Ānan sarad sudhākar sam tasu bolayé madhur dhuni bānī ।
Komal Arun kamal kumhilāyél dékhi mayéṅ ayilihuṅ jānī ।

हृदयक हार भार भेल सुबदनि नयन न होए निरोधे।
सखि सब आए खेलाओल रंग करि तसु मन किछुओ न बोधे।
Hrudayak hār bhār bhél subadani nayan na hoyé nirodhé ।
Sakhi sab āyé khélāol rang kari tasu man kichuo na bodhé ।

रगड़ल चानन मृगमद कुंकुम सभ तेजल तुअ लागी।
धनि जलहीन मीन जकँ फिरइछ अहनिस रहइछ जागी॥
Ragadal cānan mrugamad kumkum sabh téjal tua lāgī ।
Dhani jalhīn mīn jakam phirich ahanis rahaich jāgī ।।

दूतिक सुनि उपदेस सुमिरि गुन तहिखन चल्लाह धाई।
मोदवती पति राघबसिंह गति कवि विद्यापति गाई॥
Dūtik suni updés sumiri gun tahikhan callāh dhāyī ।
Modvatī pati Rāghabsimh gati kavi vidyāpati gāyī ।।

10. O! Madhava! Lord of Lakshmi!
See the condition of your beloved, separated from you:
There is no laughter on the lips,
There is no pleasant chitchat with companions,
Every moment, I am reciting your name.

Beloved! I came to see
Your face equalling the autumnal moon,
Beautiful like the red fullblown lotus,
speaking sweet words (to me).

O! Sweetfaced One!
Due to the burden in the heart (Caused by not meeting you)
the eyes cannot close in sleep:
All the companions came to play with colour
But my mind is not interested in anything.

Sandal, Kasturi, Kesar...
All adornments have been rubbed in
for your sake,
Night and day, I remain awake,
like fish swirling without water.

Hearing the message sent through the messenger,
that very moment came running
and sang, poet Vidyapati,
the servant of Raghava Singh, Lord of Modavati.

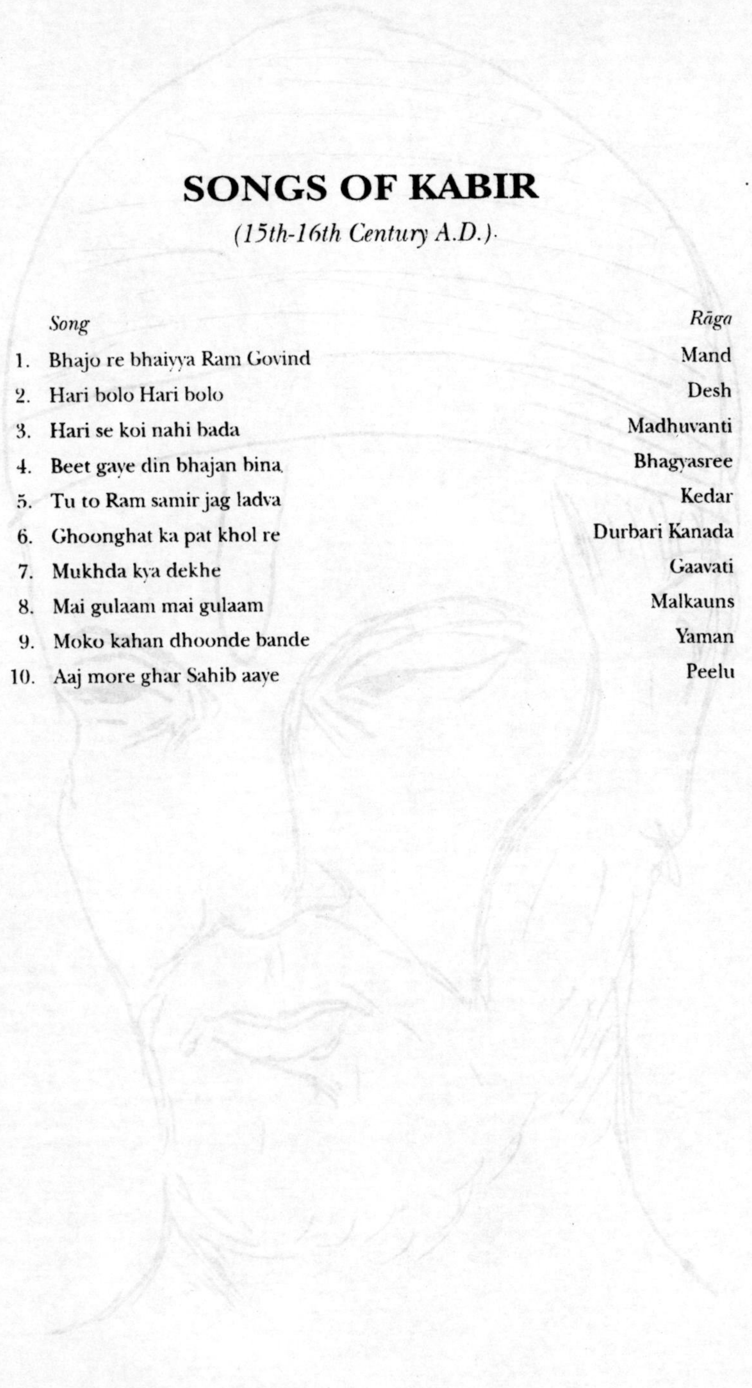

# SONGS OF KABIR

*(15th-16th Century A.D.)*

| | *Song* | *Rāga* |
|---|---|---|
| 1. | Bhajo re bhaiyya Ram Govind | Mand |
| 2. | Hari bolo Hari bolo | Desh |
| 3. | Hari se koi nahi bada | Madhuvanti |
| 4. | Beet gaye din bhajan bina | Bhagyasree |
| 5. | Tu to Ram samir jag ladva | Kedar |
| 6. | Ghoonghat ka pat khol re | Durbari Kanada |
| 7. | Mukhda kya dekhe | Gaavati |
| 8. | Mai gulaam mai gulaam | Malkauns |
| 9. | Moko kahan dhoonde bande | Yaman |
| 10. | Aaj more ghar Sahib aaye | Peelu |

*KABIR*

## KABIR (1440-1518)

Kabir, the weaver-poet-saint of Uttar Pradesh, probably lived in the fifteenth century. Scholars differ about his exact dates of birth and death.

A Muslim by birth, he found Ram in Rahim and propounded a humanistic philosophy, cutting through the conventions of caste, creed and cult.

He mostly wrote in two-line couplets, known as *dohas,* expressing his intimate love for the Almighty.

Kabir was essentially a mystic. He had no teacher. His spiritual insights and philosophical thoughts were intuitive.

Kabir's poems are contained in the *Adi Granth,* the holy scripture of the Sikhs.

The mystic songs of Kabir, preaching the omnipresence of God, and expressing a heartfelt desire for union with Him are a precious legacy of not only India, but all the world.

राग : मांड

Rāga : Mānd

1. भजो रे मन राम गोविन्द हरि
जप तप साधन कच्छु नहीं लागत
खरचत नहीं गठरी (भजो)
सन्तत सम्पत सुख के कारण
जा से भूल परी (भजो)
राम नाम को सुमिरण कर ले
सिर पे मौत खरी (भजो)
कहत कबीर सुनो भाई साधो
राम जा मुख नहीं
वह मुख धूल परी॥ (भजो)

Bhajo ré man rām govind hari
Jap tap sādhan kacchu nahī lāgat
Kharcat nahī gaṭharī
Santat sampat sukh ké kāran
Jā sé bhūl parī
Rām nām ko sumiran kar lé
Sir pé maut kharī
Kahat Kabīr sunó bhāī sādhó
Rām jā mukh nahī
Vah mukh dhūl parī

1. O! Mind! Worship Rama, Govind, Hari!
Japa (repeated recital of God's name) and
Penance (prolonged meditation)
do not cost anything;
There is no spending out of your pocket.
To think children and wealth are the means to happiness is the mistake your make.
Remember the name of Rama
Death is waiting on the wings.
Says Kabir: Listen O! Friends! O! Good men!
That face which is not turned towards Rama is worth nothing.

राग : देश

Rāga : Desh

2. हरि बोलो हरि बोलो हरि बोलो भाई
हरि न बोले वागु राम दूरायी।
काहे को पढता किण किण गीता
हरि नाम लिया सो सब कुच्छ होता।
मेरा मेरा कहकर क्या फल पाया
हरि के भजन बिना झूठक माया।
कहत कबीरा हरिगुण गाना
मावत नाशत वैकुण्ठ जाना॥

Hari bolo hari bolo hari bolo bhāyī
Hari na bolé vāgu rām dūrāyī
Kāhé ko paḍhtā kiṇ kiṇ gītā
Hari nām liyā so sab kuch hotā
Mérā mérā kahkar kyā phal pāyā
Hari ké bhajan vina jhūṭhak māyā
Kahat kabīrā hariguṇ gānā
Māvat nāśat vaikunṭh jānā

2. O! Brother! Recite the name of Hari, the Destroyer of sorrow!
Recite the name of Hari!
If you don't recite Hari's name, the Lord will be far away!
Why do you read the Gita loudly, repeatedly?
If you take Hari's name, everything happens.
What benefit did you reap, saying: "Mine, Mine!"
Without the worship of Hari, there is only false illusion.
Says Kabir: Sing the glory of Hari!
And all sins will be destroyed, and you will reach Vaikunta!
the abode of the Lord!

राग : मधुवन्ती

Rāga : Madhuvanti

3. हरि से कोई नही बड़ा दीवाने
क्येल कपलत में बड़ा
गोपी चन्दन वचन सुनकर
महाल मुल्क स्पशोडा दीवाने
हनुमान ने सेवा कीनी
ले द्रोणागिरि उठा दीवाने
प्रह्लाद बेटा हरि से लपटा
कबी काम पकड़ खटा दीवाने
पुण्डलीक ने सेवा कीनी
विट्टल इटपर टटा दीवाने
कहत कबीरा सुनो भाई साधो
हरि चरण श्रद्धा जठर दीवाने ॥

Hari sé koyi nahī badā dīwāné
Kyél kapalat mé badā
Gopī candan vacan sunkar
Mahāl mulk spaśoḍa dīwānē
Hanumān né sévā kīnī
Lé dronāgiri uṭhā dīwāné
Prahlād béṭā hari sé laptā
Kabī kām pakad khatā dīwāné
Pundalīk né sévā kīnī
Viṭṭal iṭpar ṭatā dīwāné
Kahat kabīrā sunó bhāyī sādho
Hari caraṇ śraddha jaṭhar dīwāné

3. There is no one greater than Lord Hari!
O! Mad One!

He is great in His miracles!

Hearing His sweet voice,
the Gopis gave up mansions and lands, O! Mad One!

Hanuman worshipped Him
and lifted the Dronagiri mountain, O! Mad One!

Child Prahlada, devoted to Hari
stood, holding the pillar, O! Mad One!

The lotus worshipped the Lord
and got joined to the Lord's navel, O! Mad One!

Says Kabir: Listen good brothers!
Have firm faith in the feet of Lord Hari, O! Mad One!

राग : भाग्यश्री

Rāga : Bhāgyasree

4. बीत गये दिन भजन बिना रे
Beet gayé din bhajan binā ré

बाल अवस्था खेल गँवायो।
bāl avasthā khél ganvāyó

जब जवानि तब मान घना रे (बीत गये)
jab jawāni tab mān ghanā ré

नाहि कारन मूल गंवायो।
Nāhi kāran mool ganvāyó

अजहुँ न गई मन की तृसना रे
ajahoon na gaee man kī trusnā ré

कहत कबीर सुनो भाई साधो
kahat kabir suno bhāī sādhó

पार उतर गये सन्त जना रे॥ (बीत गये)
pār utar gayé sant janā ré

4. The days have gone by without devotional singing!

Childhood was spent in play

When youth came there was the heavy load of pride

Without any reason the capital has been squandered away

Even today, the mind's desires have not disappeared!

Says Kabir: Listen, Good Brothers!

The saints have crossed over to the other bank!

राग : केदार

Rāga : Kedār

5. तू तो राम सुमिर जग लड़वा दे
Tu tó Ram sumir jag ladvā dé

कोरा कागद काली स्याही
kórā kaagad kaalee syaahī

लिखत पढ़त वाको पढ़वा दे
likhat paḍat vākó paḍvā dé

हाथी चलत है अपनी गत में
haathī chalat hai apnī gat mén

कुकुर भुकत उसको भुकवा दे।
kukur bhukt uskó bhukvādé

कहत कबीर सुनो भाई साधो
kahat Kabīr suno bhāī sādhó

नरक पचत वाको पचवा दे॥
narak pachat vāko pachvā dé

5. You devotedly recite the name of Rama, let the world fight!

There is the blank paper and the black ink

Let the learned write and read

The elephant goes its way

The dog barks, let it bark

Says Kabir: Listen, Good Brothers!
Those who like hell let them stay in hell.
(You devotedly recite the name of Rama.)

राग : दरबारी कानडा

Rāga : Durbāri Kānada

6. घुँघट का पट खोल री, तोहे पीव मिलेंगे
घट घट रमता राम रमैया,
कटुक बचन मत बोल रे।
रंग महल में दीप बरत है
आसन से मत डोल रे।
कहत कबीर सुनो भाई साधो
अनहद बाजत ढोल रे।

Ghunghaṭ ka pat khol rī, tohé piv miléngé
Ghaṭ ghaṭ ramtā rām ramaiyā
Kaṭuk bacan mat bol re
Rang mahal mén dīp barat hai
āsan sé mat dol ré
Kahat kabīr suno bhāyī sādho
Anahad bājat ḍhol ré

6. Lift your veil, then only you will meet the beloved!
Rama, the Lord is in every thing.
Don't speak harsh words!
The light is burning in the palace room (reserved for enjoyment)
Don't stir from the seat!
Says Kabir: Listen good brothers!
The eternal sound is beating.

राग : गावती

Rāga : Gāvatī

7. मुखडा क्या देखे दर्पण में
Mukhḍā kyā dekhé darpan mén
तेरे दया धर्म नहि तन में।
téré dayā dharm nahi tan mén
आम की डाली कोयलिया बोले सुगना बोले बन में।
ām kī ḍālī koyaliyā bolé suganā bolé ban mén
घरवाली तो घर में राजी फक्कड़ रानी बन में
gharwālī to ghar mén rājī phakkaḍ rānī ban mén
ऐठे धोती पाग संभारे तेल चुए जुल्फन में
aiṭé dhotī pāg sambhāré tél chué julphan mén
गली गली की सखी रिझाई दाग लगाया तन में
galī galī kī sakhī rijhāee dāg lagāyā tan mén
पाथर की एक नाव बनाई उतरा चाहे क्षन में
pāthar kī ek nāv banāyee utarā chāhé kshun mén
कहें कबीर सुनो भाई साधो ये क्या चढ़ेंगे रन में।
kahén Kabir suno bhāī sādhó yé kyā chaḍéngé ran mén

7. Why look at the face in the mirror?
   Your compassion and righteousness are not in the body.
   Let the Koel sing on the branch of the mango tree or the parrot in the forest.
   The wife is in the house, but you make merry with a queen in the woods.
   To show off your vanity, you wear a dhoti, eat sweets and apply oil on your lock of hair!
   In street after street, the courtesan captivates and leaves a stain on the body.
   You make a boat out of stone and you want to go across in a moment
   Says Kabir: Listen, good brothers! Will all this help the ascent in the final battle?

राग : मालकौंस Rāga : Mālkauns

8. मैं गुलाम मैं गुलाम मैं गुलाम तेरा
तूञ्चि मेरा सच्चा साई नाम ले ओं तेरा
रूप नहीं रंग नहीं वर्ण नहीं छाया
निर्विकार निर्गुण ही तूचि रघुराचा
एक रोटी तो लङ्गोटी द्वार तेरा पाऊँ
काम क्रोध छोड़कर हरि गुण गाऊँ
मेहरबान मेहरबान मेहर करो मेरी
दास कबीर शरण खडा नजर देख तेरी ॥

Main gulām main gulām main gulām terā
Tūnci mérā saccā sāyī nām lé om terā
Rūp nahīn rang nahin varṇ nahīn chāyā
Nirvikār nirgun hī tūci raghu rācā
Yék roṭī to langotī dwār térā pāun
Kām krodh chodkar hari gun gāun
Méharbān méharbān méhar karo merī
Dās kabīr śaran khadā najar dékh terī

8. I am your slave, I am your slave, I am your slave!
You are my true master! let me take your name!
You have no form; no colour, no shades or shadow,
You are formless, attributeless, O! King Raghava!
I can reach you, eating one roti and wearing a loincloth,
giving up lust and anger, let me sing Hari's glory,
O! Compassionate One! O! Compassionate One! show mercy on me
Servant Kabir stands seeking refuge in you, for your glance.

राग : यमन

Rāga : Yaman

9. मोको कहाँ ढूंढ़े बन्दे, में तो तेरे पास में
ना तीरथ ना सूरत में, ना एकान्त निवास में
ना मन्दिर में ना मस्जिद में, ना काशी कैलास में,
ना मैं जप में, ना मैं तप में, ना मैं बरत उपास में,
ना मैं क्रिया कर्म में रहता, नहीं जोग सन्यास में
न हीं प्राण में न हीं पिंड में, ना ब्रह्माण्ड आकाश में
ना मैं भ्रकुटा झँवर गुफा में, सब स्वासन के स्वास में
खोजो मोय तुरत मिल जाऊँ इस पल की तलास में
कहें कबीर सुनो भाई साधो, मैं तो हूँ विश्वास में॥

Moko kahān ḍhūndhé bandé, mén to téré pās mén
Nā tīrath na sūrat mén, nā yékānt nivās mén
Nā mandir mén nā masjid mén, nā kāśī kailās mén,
Nā main jap mén nā main tap mén, nā main barat upās mén,
Nā main kriyā karm mén rahtā, nahīn jog sanyās mén
Nā hīn prān mén na hīn pinḍ mén, nā brahmānd ākāś men
Nā main bhrakutajhaṅvar guphā mén, sab swāsan ké swās mén
Khojo moy turat mil jāūn ik pal kī talās mén
Kahéṅ kabīr suno bhāyī sādho, main to hūṅ viśwās men

9. Where are you searching me, friend! I am near you!

I am not in sacred rivers, not in idols, nor in solitary living,

I am not in the temple nor in the mosque, neither in Kasi nor in Kailas!

I am not in Japa, nor in penance, neither in rites nor in fasting!

I do not reside in rituals, nor in Yogic practices or renunciation (Sanyāsa)

I am not in the breath or the body, neither in the cosmos or the sky!

I am not in inaccessible caves, but in the life breath of the living!

If you search me sincerely, you will find me in a moment's search!

Says Kabir: Listen good brothers!, I am in faith!

राग : पीलू

Rāga : Peelu

10. आज मोरे घर साहिब आये
दर्शन कर दोऊ नैन जुडाये।
विगत क्लेश अखिलेश दयानिधि,
सत्य नाम निज मन्त्र सुनाये।
तिलक भाल ऊर माल मनोहर
शीश मुकुट मणिमय छबि आये।
चन्दन से चौका लिपवायो
गज मोतिन की चौक पुराये।
बाजत ताल मृदंग; झांझ डपु
साधु सन्त मिलि मंगल गाये।
दुख दरिद्र दूर सब भागे
काम क्रोध मद मोह दुराये।
भयो आनन्द भवन में चहुं दिशि
चरण कमल रज शीश चढाये।
कंचन थार संवारि आरती
घरमिन करत है हिय हलसाये
करुणा सिन्धु कबीर कृपानिधि
सत्य नाम निज मन्त्र सुनाये॥

Āj moré ghar sāhib āyé
Darśan kar doū nain judāyé
Vigat kleś akhileś dayānidhi,
Satya nām nija mantra sunāyé
Tilak bhāl ur māl manohar
Śiś mukuṭ manimay chabi āyé
Candan sé cauka lipvāyo
Gaj motin kī cauk purāyé
Bājat tāl mrudang; jhāṅjh dapu
Sādhu sant mili mangal gāyé
Dukh daridr dūr sab bhāgé
Kām krodh mad moh durāyé
Bhayo ānand bhawan mé cahuṅ diśi
Caraṇ kamal raj śīś caḍhāyé
Kancan thār saṅvāri ārti
Gharmin karat hai hiy halsāyé
Karuṇā sindhu kabīr krupānidhi
Satya nām nij mantra sunāyé

10. Today my Lord has come home.
Eyes meeting eyes, I have seen Him!
All sorrow gone, I have recited the true name, the real Mantra
to the Lord of all, the treasurehouse of mercy,
He has the tilak on the forehead,
beautiful necklace on his bosom,
His crown, full of pearls, shone like the moon.
I have smeared the precincts with sandal paste
and filled the hall with big pearls
Today, my Lord has come home.

The drums are beating
good saints are together singing auspicious songs
Sorrow and poverty have fled away far!
Lust, anger, arrogance and delusion have been removed!
Brothers! in this abode of bliss, in all quarters!
I have placed my head at the lotus feet of the Lord
In the golden plate, the aarti rides
The whole household is overwhelmed with joy!
Let us make the Ocean of mercy, treasurehouse of compassion,
Kabir's Lord listen to
the true name and the real Mantra!

# SONGS OF MEERA

*(15th-16th Century A.D.)*

| | *Song* | *Rāga* |
|---|---|---|
| 1. | Tumre karan sab sukh chode | Bhoopali |
| 2. | Mai Maine Govind leeno mol | Mand |
| 3. | Harigun gaavat naachoongee | Jayjaywanti |
| 4. | Jaago bansivare | Lalat |
| 5. | Mane chaakkar raakhojee | Misra Kapi |
| 6. | Hari Tum Haro | Durbari Kanada |
| 7. | Pag Ghunghroo bandh Meera naachee | Malkauns |
| 8. | Mere to Giridhar Gopal | Jinjoti |
| 9. | Baso mere nainan men Nandlal | Peelu |
| 10. | Paayojee maine | Pahadi |

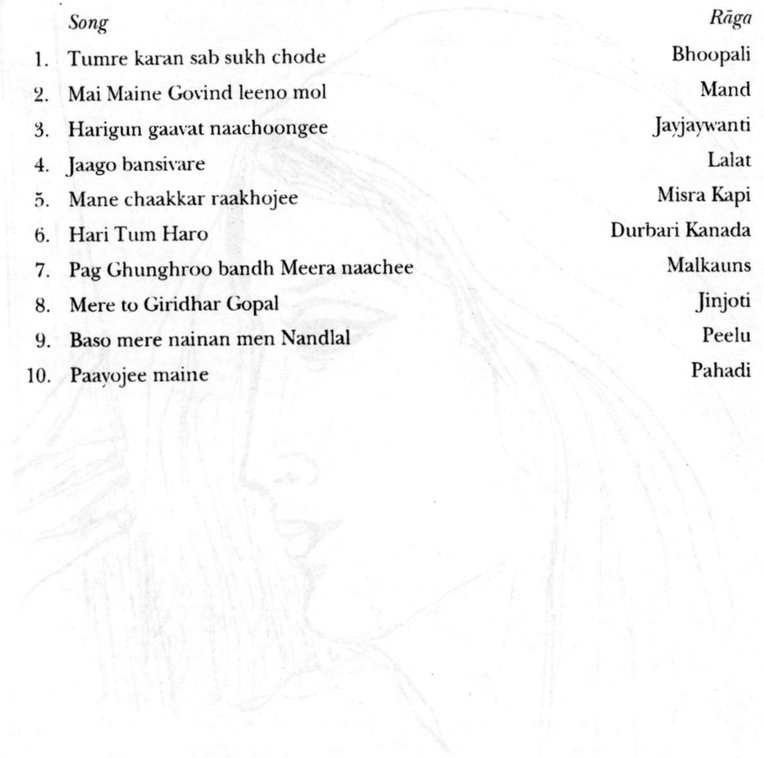

*MEERA*

## MEERA (1498-1547)

Meera, the princess-poet, saint-singer, was born in 1498 in a royal family of Mewar, Rajasthan.

From childhood she became a devotee of Krishna.

She was married to Bhojaraja, a son of Rana Sanga who died while quite young.

Early widowhood helped Meera in her God-oriented ascetic life of prayer and devotion.

Like Andal of the seventh century, Meera saw herself as the bride of the Lord (Krishna) and poured forth her spiritual yearnings in soulful poetry.

Persecuted by her husband's brother, Meera had to leave Chittor and go to Brindavan. Her last few years were spent in Dwaraka, Gujarat. She died in 1547 A.D.

The God-intoxicated songs of Meera have transcended regional barriers and are sung all over India.

राग : भूपाली — Rāga : Bhoopāli

1. तुमरे कारण सब सुख छोडा
Tumré kāran sab sukh cchodā

अब मोहीं क्यूँ तरजाओ हो
ab mohīn kyon tarzaaó hó

बिरह बिथा लागो उर अन्तर
birah bithā laago ur antar

सो तुम आये बुझावो हो
so tum aayé bujhāvó hó

अब छोड़त नही बनै प्रभुजी
ab cchodat nahi banai Prabhujī

हँसकर तुरंत बुलाओ हो
hanskar turant bulaavó hó

मीरा दासी जनम जनम की
Meera daasee janam janam kī

अंग से अंग लगाओ हो ॥
ang se ang lagaaó hó

1. For your sake, I gave up all pleasures

Now why are you making me long for you?

Create the pang of separation inside the bosom

so that you can come and quench it

O! Lord! now I will not leave you

Smilingly, call me soon!

Meera is your servant in birth after birth

Unite me with you in every limb.

राग : मांड Rāga : Mānd

2. माई मैंने गोविन्द लीनो मोल।
गोविन्द लीनो मोल।
Māi mainé Govind leenó mól
Govind leenó mól

कोई कहे सस्ता, कोई कहे महँगा
लीनो तराजू तोल।
Koi kahé sastā, koi kahé mahangā
leeno tarājū tól

कोई कहे घर में, कोई कहे बन में
राधा के संग खिलोल।
Koi kahé ghar mén, koi kahé ban mén
Rādhā ké sang khilol

मीरा के प्रभु गिरिधर नागर,
आवत प्रेम के डोल।
Meera ké Prabhu Giridhar Nāgar
āvat prem ké dól

2. Mother, I have bargained and bought Govinda!

Let some say: Cheap!, let some say: Costly!
I have weighed in the balance.

Let some say: He is in the house, some say: in the woods!
Sporting in the company of Radha!

When Meera's Lord Giridhar Krishna comes, love swings!

राग : जयजयवन्ती Rāga : Jayjaywanti

3. हरि गुण गावत नाचूंगी
Harigunạ gāvat naachoongee

प्रभु गुण गावत नाचूंगी
Prabugunạ gāvat naachoongee

अपने मंदिर मों बैठ बैठकर
apné mandir mon baiṭ baiṭkar

गीता भागवत बाचूंगी
Geeta bhāgavat baachoongee

ज्ञान ध्यान की, गठडी बांधकर
jnān dhyān kī gaṭaḍī bāndhkar

हरि हर संग मैं लागूंगी।
Hari har sang main lāgoongee

मीरा कहे प्रभु गिरिधर नागर
Meera kahé Prabhu Giridhar Nāgar

सदा प्रेमरस चाखूंगी॥
Sadā premras chaakhoongee

3. I will dance singing the glories of Hari!

I will dance singing the glories of the Lord!

Sitting in my own temple

I will read the Gita and the Bhagavata!

Making a bundle of knowledge and meditation,

I will stick to the company of Hari!

Says Meera: I shall always enjoy the feeling of love
towards my Lord Giridhar Krishna!

राग : ललत

Rāga : Lalat

4. जागो बन्सीवरे ललना (जागो)

जागो मेरे प्यारे

jaago bansivaré lalanā

jaago mérĕ pyāré

रजनी बीति भोर भयो है

rajani beeti bhor bhayo hai

घर घर खुले किवारे

ghar ghar khulé kivaaré

गोपी दहि मथत सुनियत है

gopī dahi mathat suniyat hai

कंकना के झनकार

kankanā ké jhankaar

उठो, लालजी भोर भयो है

uthó lāljee bhor bhayo hai

सुर नर ठाडे द्वारे

sur nar ṭāḍé dwāré

ग्वाल बाल सब करत कुलाहल

gvaal baal sab karat kulāhal

जय जय शब्द उच्छारे

jay jay sabd ucchaaré

माखन रोटी हाथ में लीनी

mākhan rotī hāth men leenee

गौवन के रखवारे

gauvan ké rakhvaaré

मीरा के प्रभु गिरिधर नागर

Meera ké Prabhu Giridhar Naagar

शरण आया को तारे।

saraṇ aayaa kó taaré ।

4. Wake up! O! Darling with the flute!
Wake up my Beloved!

The night is over, morning has come
In every household doors are open

One can hear the cowherdesses churning the curds
the jingling of bangles

Wake up, O! Lord! it is already morning!
The angels are standing at the doorstep

The cowboys are making noises
and shouting: Hail! Hail!,
taking bread and butter in their hands,
O! protector of cows!

O! Meera's Lord! Giridhar!
I have come seeking refuge! Protect me!

राग : मिश्र-कापी — Rāga : Misra-Kāpi

5\. मने चाकर राखो जी — Mané cākar rākho jī

A. मने चाकर राखो जी,
मने चाकर राखो जी॥

mané cākar rākho jī
mané cākar rākhojī

B. चाकर रहसूं बाग लगासूं,
नित उठ दरसन पासूं।
बृन्दावन की कुंज गलिन में,
तेरी लीला गासूं॥
मने चाकर राखो जी॥

Cākar rahasūn bāg lagāsūn,
nit uṭh darsan pāsūṅ
brundāvan kī kunj galin méṅ,
térī līlā gāsūṅ
mané cākar rākho jī

C. मोर मुकुट पीताम्बर सोहे
गल बैजन्ती माला।
वृन्दावन में धेनु चरावे,
मोहन मुरली वाला॥
मने चाकर राखो जी॥

Mor mukuṭ pītambar sohé
Gal baijantī mālā
Vrundāvan méṅ dhénu carāvé,
mohan muralī wālā
mané cākar rākho jī

D. जोगी आया जोग करन कू,
तप करणे सन्यासी।
हरि भजन कू साधू आयो,
वृन्दावन के बासी॥
मने चाकर राखो जी॥

jogī āyā jog karan kū,
tap karaṇé sannyāsī
hari bhajan kū sādhū āyo,
Vrundāvan ké bāsi
mané cākar rakho jī

E. 'मीरा' के प्रभु गहिर गंभीरा,
हृदय रहो जी धीरा।
आधी रात प्रभु दरशण दैहें,
प्रेम नदी के तीरा॥
मने चाकर राखो जी॥

'mīrā' ké prabhu gahir gambhīrā,
hruday raho jī dhīrā
ādhī rāt prabhu darśaṇ daihéṅ,
prém nadī ké tīrā
mané cākar rakho jī

5.A. O! Lord! Keep me as your servant
Keep me as your servant.

B. Remaining a servant, I shall plant gardens,
Daily I shall get up and see you.
In the forest paths of Brindavan I shall sing of your exploits.
Lord! Keep me as your servant.

C. Wearing the peacock crest, yellow silken robe
and the chrysanthemum garland on the neck
The Enchanting One with the flute
herds the cows in Brindavan.

D. Yogis will come to do yoga
Sages will come to do penance
The good people of Brindavan will come
to sing bhajans of Hari.
Lord! keep me as your servant.

E. Meera's Lord is great
O! Heart, be patient and brave.
At midnight, on the banks of the beloved river (Yamuna)
The Lord will appear.
Lord! Keep me as your servant.

राग : दरबारी कानडा Rāga : Durbāri Kānadā

6. हरि तुम हरौ जन की पीर

हरि तुम हरौ जन की पीर।
द्रौपदी की लाज राखी तुम बढायो चीर॥
भक्त कारन रूप नरहरि धर्‌यौ आप सरीर।
हिरनकस्यप मार लीन्हों धर्‌यौ नाहीं धीर॥
बूडतो गजराज राख्यौ कियो बाहर नीर।
दासी मीरा लाल गिरधर दुख जहां तहां पीर॥

Harī Tum harau jan kī pīr
Hari tum harau jan kī pīr
draupadī kī lāj rākhī tum baḍhāyo cīr
bhakt kāran rūp narhari dharyau āp sarīr
hirankasyap mār līnhoṅ dharyau nahīn dhīr
būḍto gajrāj rākhyau kiyo bāhar nīr
dāsī mīrā lāl girdhar dukh jahāṅ tahāṅ pīr

*The Pandavas were lured into a game of dice by their enemies and cousins, the Kauravas. King Yudhishtira, Head of the Pandavas, pledged one thing after another and lost. Draupadi, the wife, was the last item pledged and lost. To humiliate the Pandavas, Draupadi was dragged into the assembly and sought to be disrobed in public by Dussasana. Krishna, in response to Draupadi's prayer, lengthened her robe to such an extent that Dussasana, who was pulling at it, fell exhausted. This episode is a well known and a classic example of Krishna's timely help to distressed devotees.

6. O! Hari, Destroyer of sorrow! You dispel the sorrow of people.

You protected Draupadi's* modesty by increasing the length of her robe.

For the sake of your devotee, you wore the form of Man-lion** and killed Hiranyakasipu.

You protected the Elephant King*** by bringing him out of water.

O! Holder of mountain! How long has your servant Meera to wait in sorrow?

**The demon, Hiranyakasipu, got a boon from Brahma that he could not be killed by any god, man or beast. His arrogance knowing no limits Hiranyakasipu usurped all regions and proved a threat to the cosmos. His son, Prahlada, saintly by disposition, was an ardent devotee of God. This displeased Hiranyakasipu. Angrily he asked his son "Where is your God?" and struck a pillar in front with his sword. Out of the pillar burst forth a form which was neither man nor beast. It was the form of a man-lion, fierce and frightening! The man-lion took Hiranyakasipu on his lap and tore him to death drinking his blood.

***Indradyumna, a king of Pandya land, was cursed to become an elephant by Agastya, since immersed in God worship, the king forgot to offer hospitality to the sage. One day the elephant king entered a lake to drink water. There dwelt in that very lake a celestial being (Gandharva) cursed to be a crocodile. The crocodile attacked the elephant king, who prayed to Vishnu, who came down on the back of Garuda and rescued the elephant, cutting asunder the crocodile with His discus. Both the crocodile and the elephant got back their old forms.

राग : मालकौंस

Rāga : Malkauns

7. पग घुंघरु बांध मीरा नाची रे
मैं तो अपने नारायण को हो गई आप ही दासी रे

विष का प्याला राणाजी ने भे

पीवत मीरा हांसी रे

लोग कहें मीरा भई बावरो

नाति कहैं कुल नासी रे

मीरा कहे प्रभु गिरिधर नागरु

सहज मिले अविनासी रे ॥

Pag ghunghru bāndh mīrā nācī re
main to apne nārāyaṇ ko ho gaī
āp hī dāsī re
viṣ ka pyālā rāṇajī ne bhe
pīvat mīrā hāṅsī re
log kaheṅ mīrā bhaī bāvaro
nāti kahaiṅ kul nāsī re
mīrā kahe prabhu giridhar nāgaru
sahaj mile avināsī re

7. Wearing anklets on her feet, Meera is dancing,

I have become the servant of my own Narayana.

The Rana sent the cup of poison,

Meera drinks it smilingly.

Let people say Meera is mad!

Let relations say she is destroyer of the family!

Meera says she has got the indestructible
company of Lord Krishna, the holder of the mountain.

राग : जिंजोटी

Rāga : Jinjoti

8. मेरे तो गिरिधर गोपाल
दूसरो न कोई।
जाके सिर मोर मुकुट मेरो पति सोई-प्रभु
शंख चक्र गदा पद्म कंठ माला कोई
तात मात बंधु भ्रात अपना न कोई
छांड दई कुल को कान, का करेगा हे कोई
असुवन जल सींचि सींचि प्रेम बेल बोई
दासी मीरा प्रभु लगन लगी अब मोहीं
मेरे तो गिरिधर गोपाल
दूसरो न कोई॥

ḿere to giridhar gopāl
dūsro na koī
jāke sir mor mukut mero pati soī-prabhu
sankh cakr gadā padma kanṭh mālā koī
tāt māt bandhu bhrāt apnā na koī
chānḍ daī kul ko kān, ka taregā hé koī
asuvan jal sīnci sīnci prem ḃel boī
dāsī mīrā prabhu lagan lagī ab mohīṅ
méré to giridhar gopāl
dūsro na koī

8. Gopala, the cowherd, the holder of the mountain is mine,
No one else.

My master wears the peacock feathers in his crown and holds the conch, discus and the mace. He has the garland of lotuses on his neck.

I have no father, no mother, relatives or brothers.
I have broken family ties; who can do anything?

I have spoken of my love through my tears.

Servant Meera has fallen in love with the Lord. He is now mine.
Gopala is mine. No one else!

राग : पीलू

Rāga : Peelu

9. बसो मोरे नैनन में नन्दलाल
मोहनी मूरत, सांवरी सूरत, नैना बने बिसाल।
मोर मुकुट मकराकृति कुण्डल अरुण तिलक सोहे भाल।
अधर सुधा रस मुरली राजत, ऊर बैजंती माल
छुद्र घंटिका कटि तट शोभित, नूपुर सवद रसाल
मीरा प्रभु संतन सुखदाई भगत बऊल गोपाल॥

Baso moré nainan méṅ nand lāl
mohanī mūrat sāṅvarī sūrat, nainā bané bisāl
mor mukuṭ makarākruti kundal aruṅ tilak sohé bhāl
adhar sudha ras muralī rājat, ūr baijantī māl
chudr ghantikā kaṭi taṭ śobhit, nūpur sawad rasāl
mīrā prabhu santan sukhadāī bhagat baūl gopāl

9. Reside in my eyes, O! Darling son of Nanda!

Your form is captivating, as are your cloudhued complexion and wide eyes!

You have the peacock crest, ear-ornaments shaped like the crocodile and the crimson mark on your forehead.

With your lips you play the flute and give nectarlike music,

On your chest shines the chrysanthemum garland,

Your waist is radiant with the girdle of tiny bells,

and your feet sound sweet with the jingling of the anklets.

Your are the Lord of Meera, you bestow bliss on saints,

O! Protector of cows! You affectionately look after your devotees.

राग : पहाडी Rāga : Pahādi

10. पायो जी मैंने राम-रतन धन पायो।
वस्तु अमोलिक दी मेरे सतगुरु
किरपा कर अपनायो।
Pāyó jī mainé Rām ratan dhan pāyó
vastu amolik dī méré satguru
kirapā kar apanāyó

जनम जनम की पूँजी पाई,
जगमें सभी खोवायो।
janam janam kī poonjī pāyī
jag mén sabhī khovāyó

खरचै न खूटै, वाको चोर न लूटै,
दिन दिन बढ़त सवायो।
kharachai na khūtai, vāko chor na lootai
din din baḍat savāyó

सत की नाव, खेवटिया सतगुरु
भवसागर तर आयो।
sat kī nāv, khévatiyā satguru
bhavasāgar tar āyó

मीरा के प्रभु गिरिधर नागर
हरख हरख जस गायो।
Meerā ké Prabhu Giridhar Nāgar
harakh harakh jas gāyo

10. I have obtained the wealth of diamonds that is Rama!
My good teacher gave me an invaluable thing and
I have made it my own!

I have obtained the accumulated capital of several births
after searching in the entire universe!

The expenditure does not have to stop,
thieves will not rob,
Day by day the enjoyment increases!

The boat is truth, the good teacher is the boatman
I have come to cross the ocean of samsara!

Meera's Lord Giridhar will be pleased
I have sung of His glory!

# SONGS OF PURANDHARADASA

*(15th-16th Century A.D.)*

| | *Song* | *Rāga* |
|---|---|---|
| 1. | Ninna dhyaanava kodo | Vibhas |
| 2. | Devabanda | Durga |
| 3. | Paraakumaadade | Saveri |
| 4. | Innudaya barade | Kalyanavasantam |
| 5. | Hari Narayana | Kedaram |
| 6. | Narayana ninna naamada | Suddha dhanyasi |
| 7. | Kandu Kandu | Ragamalika (Sahana, Mohanam, Bhairavi) |
| 8. | Maraya beda | Ragesvari |
| 9. | Kelano Hari | Poorvakalyani |
| 10. | Rama Rama Rama Rama Rama yenniro | Vasanta |

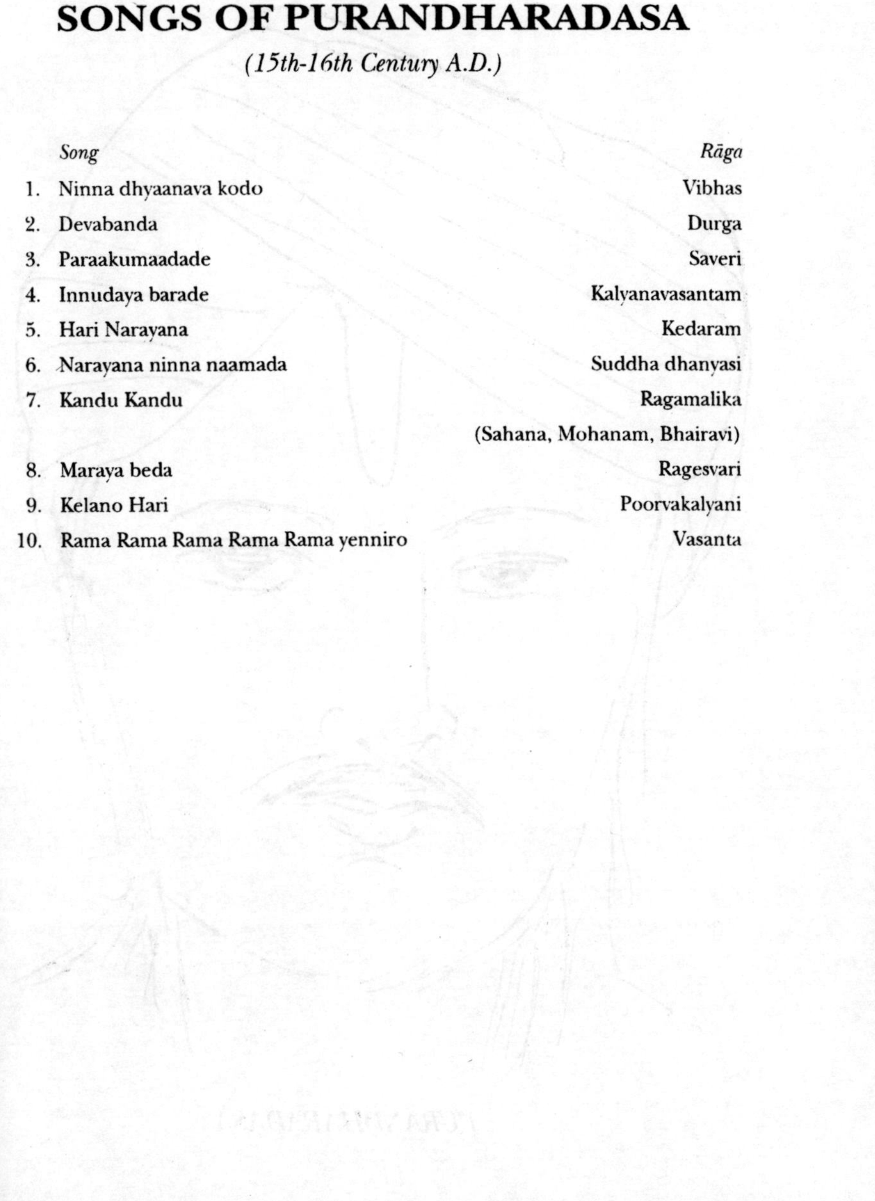

*PURANDHARADASA*

## PURANDHARADASA (1484-1564)

Purandharadasa, the Kannada saint-musician, was actually a Maratha by birth. He was born in a village near Pune in 1484, the son of a banker.

As a boy, he learnt music and Sanskrit; growing up was married to Saraswatibai, got involved in making money.

Suddenly one day, due to a miracle, the young banker renounced everything and left for Pandharpur and got initiated into asceticism. He travelled to various temples and pilgrim centres all over India and composed devotional songs numbering thousands.

Purandharadasa is considered the Grandfather of Carnatic music. About 8000 of his musical compositions survive today. Purandharadasa's songs extol the mercy of God and are immersed in intense devotion, though replete with references to myths and legends of Sri Krishna.

Having lived a full life of prolific creativity, Purandharadasa died in 1564 at the age of eighty.

Purandharadasa illustrated through his life Tyagaraja's dictum that music and devotion combined make the best path to God-realisation.

राग : विभास

Rāga : Vibhās

1. निन्न ध्यानव कोडो एन्न धन्यन माडो
पन्नगशयन श्री पुरन्धर विटल।
अम्बुजनयनने अम्बुज जनकने
अम्बुजनाभ श्री पुरन्धर विटल (निन्न)
पङ्कजनयनने पङ्कज जनकने
पङ्कजनाभ श्री पुरन्धर विटल (निन्न)
भागीरतीपित भागवतप्रिय
योगिकळरसन श्री पुरन्धर विटल (निन्न)

Ninna dhyānava kodo énna dhanyana mādó
Pannagasayana sree Purandhara Vittala
Ambujanayanané ambujajanakané (Ninna)
Ambujanābha sree Purandhara Vittala
Pankajanayanané Pankajajanakané
Pankajanābha sree Purandhara Vittala (Ninna)
Bhagīrathīpita Bhāgavatapriya
Yogikaḷarasana sree Purandhara Vittala (Ninna)

1. *Ninna dhyānava kodo*

Grant me meditation on you and make me blessed

O! Purandhara Vittala! who lies on the serpent!

O! Lotuseyed One! who created the lotus!

O! Purandhara Vittala! who has the lotus in the navel!

(Grant me...)

O! Lotuseyed One! who created the lotus!

O! Purandhara Vittala! who has the lotus in the navel

(Grant me...)

O! Father of Bhagirati! Fond of the Bhavagata!

Who pleases yogis! O! Purandhara Vittala! (Grant me...)

राग : दुर्गा

Rāga : Durga

2. देव बंदा नम्म स्वामि बंदानो

Déva bandā namma swāmi bandaanó

देवर देव शिरोमणि बंदानो

Dévara Déva sirómaṇi bandaanó

उरगशायन बंद गरुडगमन बंद

Uragasāyana banda Garudagamana banda

नरगोलिदव बंद नारायण बंद ॥

Naragólidava banda Nārāyana banda

मंदरोद्धर बंद मा मनोहर बंद

Mandaroddhara banda mā manohara banda

वृंदावनपति गोविंद बंदानो

Varindāvanapati Govinda bandaanó

नक्रहरनु बंद चक्रधरनु बंद

Nakraharanu banda chakradharanu banda

अक्रूरगोलिद तिविक्रम बंदानो

Akruragolida Trivikrama bandaanó

पक्षिवाहन बंद लक्ष्मणाग्रज बंद

Pakshivāhana banda Lakshmanāgraja banda

अक्षजफलद श्री लक्ष्मीरमण बंद

Akshajaphalada srī Lakshmīramana banda

निगमगोचर बंद नित्यतृप्तनु बंद

Nigamagóchara banda Nityatriptanu banda

नगेमुख पुरंधरविठल बंदानो ॥

Nagémukha Purandhara Viṭala bandaanó

2. *Déva bandā*

The Lord has come, our Master has come!

The God of gods who wears the crestjewel has come!

The Lord who lies on the serpent and rides Garuda, has come!

The destroyer of Demon Naraka, Narayana, the abode of all beings has come!

The one who rescued Mandara has come! Our Charming One has come!

The Lord of Vrindavan, Govinda has come!

The One who killed the crocodile has come, the holder of the discus has come!

The destroyer of demon Akrura has come, Trivikrama, the victor of three worlds has come!

The One whose vehicle is the bird (Garuda) has come!
The elder brother of Lakshmana has come!

The granter of immortality, the Lord of Lakshmi has come!

The one who permeates the Vedas has come, the Ever-satisfied One has come!

Purandhara Vittala, facing the mountain, has come!

राग : सावेरि

Rāga : Saveri

3. ''पराकु माडदे''

प. पराकु माडदे परामरिसि ऐन्न
अपराधंगळ क्षमिसो (परा)

अ. दरारमण फणिदरामरर्चित
सुराधिपतिविधि हरादि वन्दित (परा)

''Parāku māḍadé''

P. Parāku māḍadé parāmarisi enna
Aparādhangaḷa kṣamiso (Parā)

A. Darāramaṇa phaṇidarāmararcita
Surādhi pativiḍhi harādi vandita (Parā)

च.1. नर रोळगे पामरनु नानिह
पर रिगे साधन नानरिये श्री हरिये
शरणु होक्के निन्न चरण कमलक्के
करुणदि निन्न स्मरणे एनगित्तु (परा)

C.1. Nara roḷage pāmaranu nāniha
Para rigé sādhana nānariyé śrī hariyé
Śaraṇu hokké ninna caraṇa kamalakké
Karuṇadi ninna smaraṇé énagittu (Parā)

च.2. जपव नानरियेनु तपव नानरियनु
उपवास व्रतगळ नरिये श्री हरिये
कृपावलोक दिन्द आपापगळनेल्ल
अपाहतव माडो अपार महिमने (परा)

C.2. Japava nānariyenu tapava nānariyanu
Upavāsa vratagaḷa nariyé śrī hariyé
Krupāvaloka ḍinḍa āpāpagaḷanella
Apāhatava mādo apāra mahimané (Parā)

च.3. करिय रक्षिसि द्रौपदिय वालिसि
तरुळ्न कोलिदु नी पोरदे दयादि
सिरिय रस निन्न सरियारु काणे
करुणिसय्या श्री पुरन्दर विठल (परा)

C.3. Kariya rakṣisi draupadiya vālisi
Taruḷana kolidu nī poradé dayādi
Siriya rasa ninna sariyāru kāṇé
Karuṇisayyā śrī purandara viṭhala

3. *Paraaku maadadé*

You do no lose anything by being kind to me.
Forgive all my faults.

O! Darling of earth (Lord of Bhoodevi)!
Worshipped by Adisesha, wearer of thousand hoods!
venerated by Indra, Chief of angels and Siva!

C.1. Here I am, a sinner among men
O! Hari! Destroyer of sorrow! I do not know
the means by which one can cross over to the other world.
I surrender at your lotus feet
Be kind and bestow on me remembrance of only you.

C.2. I do not know Japa (Chanting of names)
I do not know penance,
O! Hari! Destroyer of sorrow! I do not know
fasting and other rituals.
With your kind glance, remove all my sins,
O! Lord, whose greatness is limitless!

C.3. You protected the elephant, you heard Draupadi's wail
You looked after Prahlada, with compassion, You are the unrivalled Ruler
I do not see anyone who could be your equal
Please be kind towards me, O! Lord of Purandhara!

राग : कल्याण वसन्तम् Rāga : Kalyāna vasantam

4. "इन्नूदय बारदे"

प. इन्नूदय बारदे दासन मेले
इन्नूदय बारदे (इन्नू)
अ. पन्नग शयन श्री परम पुरुष हरिये (इन्नू)

"Innūdaya bāradé"

P. Innūdaya bāradé dāsana mélé
Innūdaya bāradé (Innū)
A. Pannaga śayana śrī parama puruṣa hariyé (Innū)

च.1. नाना देशगळल्लि नाना कालगळल्लि
नाना योनिगळल्लि नलिदु पुट्टि
नानु नन्नदु एंब नरक दोळगे बिद्दु
नीने गतियेन्दु नंबिद दासन मेले (इन्नू)

C.1. Nānā deśagaḷalli nānā kālagaḷalli
Nānā yonigaḷalli nalidu putti
Nānu nannadu émba naraka doḷagé biddu
Nīné gatiyendu nambida dāsana mélé

च.2. मनोवाक्काय दिन्द माडुवे कर्मगळेल्ल
दान वन्तक निनगे दानवित्ते
येनु माडिदरेनु प्राण निन्नदे स्वामि
श्री नाथ पुरन्दर विठल दासन मेले (इन्नू)

C.2. Manovākkāya dinda māduvé karmagaḷélla
Dāna vantaka ninagé dānavitté
Yénu mādidarénu prāṇa ninnadé swāmi
Śrī nātha purandara viṭhala dāsan mélé (Innū)

4. *Innudaya bāradé*

Are you yet to get kindly disposed towards me?
This servant of yours?
Are you yet to get kindly disposed?

O! Hari! Destroyer of sorrow! You, who are the supreme person! and sleep on the serpent (Adisesha)!

C.1. In various countries, at various times,
In various wombs, I have taken birth,
In this hell of "I and mine", I have fallen,
This servant of yours believes that You are the only refuge
Are you yet to get kindly disposed?

C.2. Through mind, speech and body, I do my duty,
I have given alms to you, the Giver,
In whatever I have done, O! Master! the lifebreath is yours
O! Lord of Lakshmi! O! Lord of Purandhara!
Towards this servant of yours,
Are you yet to get kindly disposed?

राग : केदार

Rāga : Kédar

5. हरि नारायण हरि नारायण

प. हरि नारायण हरि नारायण
हरि नारायण एनु मनवे
नारायणनेम्ब नाम बीजव
नारद बित्तिदद धरयोळगे (हरि)
Hari Nārāyaṇa hari nārāyaṇa
hari nārāyaṇa yénu manavé
nārāyaṇémba nāma bījawa
Nārada bittdida dharayolagé (Hari)

च.1. तरुलध्रुवनिन्द अंकुरिसितु अदु
वरप्रह्लादनिन्द मोलकायितु
धरणीश रुक्मांगदनिन्द चिगुरितु
गुरुपितामहनिन्द हूवायितु (हरि)
taruladhruvaninda ankurisitu adu
varaprahladaninda molakāyitu
dharaṇīśa rukmāngadaninda ciguritu
gurupitamahaninda hūvāyitu (Hari)

च.2. विजयन सतियिन्द कायायितु अदु
गजेन्द्रनिन्द तोर हण्णायितु
द्विज शुकमुनियिन्द फलपक्व वायितु
अजामिल तानुण्डु रस सहित (हरि)
vijayana satiyinda kāyāyitu adu
gajéndraninda tora hannāyitu
dwija śukamuniyinda phalapakwa vāyitu
ajāmila tānuṇḍu rasa sahita (Hari)

च.3. कामित फलवेम्बो नाम ओन्दिरलागि
होम नेम जपतप याके
स्वामि श्री पुरन्दर विठल रायन
नेमदिन्दलि नी नेन मनवे (हरि)
kāmita phalavémbo nāma ondiralāgi
homa néma japatapa yāké
swāmi śrī purandara viṭhala rāyana
némadindali nī néna manavé (Hari)

5. *Hari Nārāyaṇa*

O! Mind! Chant the name of Hari Narayana!
Narada sowed the seed of the name: "Narayana"
in mother earth.

C.1. Through the child Dhruva* it sprouted;
It became a seedling by the prayer of Prahlada;
Through King Rukmangada, it grew further
Through Bhishma (Guru Pitamaha) it flowered.

C.2. Through Arjuna's spouse, Draupadi, it bore fruit
Through Gajendra, the elephant king, the fruit became ripe;
Through the sage Suka, it became totally ripe,
And Ajamila ate it up with its essence.

C.3. When the name alone brings the desired result,
Why take resort to Homa, Japa and penance?
O! Mind! Remember always the name of the Lord,
Purandhara's Master!

*King Uttanapada had two wives: Suruchi and Suniti. Suruchi was the favourite of the King. Dhruva was Suniti's son, while Uttama was Suruchi's. One day, seeing Uttama seated on his father's lap, Dhruva also wanted to climb on the King's lap, but he was abused and turned away by Suruchi. Dhruva went crying to his mother, who advised him to worship the Lord to get whatever he desired. Dhruva, only five years in age, but highly sensitive, went to the forest and prayed, guided by sage Narada. The Lord appeared before Dhruva and blessed him. Dhruva returned triumphantly and ruled his country efficiently for long and ultimately merged in the Supreme. He is in popular belief identified as the pole star.

राग : शुद्ध धन्याशि Rāga : Śuddha dhanyāśi

6. ''नारायण निन्न नामद''

प. नारायण, नारायण, नारायण, निन्न नामद स्मरणेय
सारामृतवु एन्न नाळिगेगे भरदि

''Nārāyaṇa ninna nāmada''

P. Nārāyaṇa nārāyaṇa nārāyaṇa ninna nāmada smaraṇeya
Sārāmrutavu énna nāḷigégé bharadī

च.1. कष्टदल्लिरळि उत्कृष्टदल्लिरलि
येष्टादरु मतिकेट्टु इरलि
कृष्ण कृष्ण एन्दो शिष्टरु बेडुव
अष्टाक्षर मद मन्त्रर नामद (नारा)

C.1. Kaṣṭadalliraḷi utkruṣṭadallirali
Yéṣṭādaru matikeṭṭu irali
Kriṣṇa kriṣṇa éndo śiṣṭaru béduva
Aṣṭākṣara mada mantrara nāmada (Nārā)

च.2. सन्तत हरि निन्न सासिरनामवेन्न
अन्तरंगदलि इति श्री
यन्तो पुरन्दर विठल रायन
अन्त्यकालदलि सोबगे (नारा)

C.2. Santata hari ninna sāsiranāmāvenna
Antarangadali iti śrī
Yanto purandara vithala rāyana
Antyakāladali sobagé (Nārā)

6. *Nārāyaṇa ninna naamada*

O! Narayana! Abode of all beings!
Let the recitation of your name, Narayana,
and the nectar of its essence come to my tongue easily!

C.1. When one is in trouble or in a happy state,
in mental peace or mental aberration,
good persons crave for the name: Krishna,
or the eightlettered Mantra: Om namo Narayana.

C.2. O! Hari! Destroyer of sorrow!
Always let your thousand names
be in my heart!
If the name of Purandhara's Master is remembered
at the final hour of life, there will be true elevation.

राग : रागमालिका Rāga : Ragamalika

7. कण्डु कण्डु

प. कण्डु कण्डु नी एन्न कै बिडुवरे, (सहाना)
कृष्णा पुण्डरीकाक्ष श्री पुरुषोत्तम (क)

P. kandu kandu nī yénna kai biḍuvare
krushna punḍarīkākṣa śrī puruṣottama (ka)

च.1. बन्दुगळु एनगिल्ल वदुकिनलि
सुखविल्ल निन्देयलि नोन्देनय्या
नीरजाक्ष बन्धुबळगवु नीने
तन्देतायु नीने। एन्देन्दु निन्ने
नंबिदेनु श्री कृष्ण॥

C.1. bandugaḷu yénagilla vadukinali
sukhavilla nindéyali nondénayyā
nīrajākṣa bandhu baḷagavu nīné
tandé tāyu nīné yéndendu ninné
nambidénu śrí kruṣṇa

च.2. क्षणवोन्दु युगवागि तृणकिन्त कडेयागि (मोहनं)
येणिसवळवल्ल ईभवद व्यथेय
सनकादि मुनिवन्दय वनज संभव जनक
फणिशायि प्रह्लाद गोलिद श्री कृष्ण

C.2. kṣaṇavondu yugavāgi truṇakinṭa kadéyāgi
yénisavaḷavalla yī bhavda vyathéya
sanakādi munivandya vanaja sambhava janaka
phaṇiśāyi prahlāda golida śrī kriṣṇa

च.3. भक्तवत्सलनेंबो बिरुदु पोत्तिद मेले (भैरवी)
भक्तपरादीननागि इरबेडवे
मुक्तिदायक नीनु होन्नूर पुरवास
शक्तगुरु पुरन्दर विठल श्रीकृष्णा (क)

C.3. bhakta vatsalanémbo birudu pottida mélé
bhaktaparā dīnanagi yirabédavé
muktidāyaka nīnu honnūra puravāsa
śaktaguru purandara vithala Śrī Kriṣṇa (ka)

7. *Kandu kandu*

Are you, knowingly, giving up my hand?
O! Krishna! Pundarikaksha! Sree Purushottama?

C.1. I have no relations in this life,
There is no joy in regretting this and suffering!
You Lotuseyed One! You are my relations,
my father and mother.
O! Krishna! I always depend on you.

C.2. A moment becomes an eon, yet is worthless than grass.
We cannot count the afflictions of the phenomenal world,
O! Krishna! You blessed sages like Sanaka, lotusborn Brahma,
Prahlada, O! Lord lying on the serpent Adisesha!
(Bless me too!)

C.3. Since you have the title of being the darling of your devotees,
Should you not be kind to this devotee?
You are the granter of liberation!, O! Lord who live in Honnur!
O! Sree Krishna! O! Powerful Teacher! Master of Purandhara!

राग : रागेश्वरी

Rāga : Ragesvari

8. मरय बेडा मनवे नीनु हरिय स्मरणेय
Maraya béda manavé nīnu hariya smaranéya

यागयज्ञ माडलेके योगि यतियु आगलेके
Yāgayajna maadléké yogi yatiyu aagaléke

नागशयन नारद वन्द्यन कूगि भजने माडु बेगा।
Nagasayana Narada vandyana koogi bhajané mādu bégā

सतियु सुतरु हितरु नन्नु मतियु केट्टु केडलि बेडा।
गतियु तप्पि होगुवागे सतियु सुतरु बरुबरेनो।
Satiyusutaru hitaru nannu matiyu kettu kédali bédā
Gatiyu tappi hoguvāge satiyusutaru barubaréno

हरि स्मरणे मात्रदिन्त घोर दुरितवेल्ल नाश
परम पुरुष पुरन्दरविट्टल पदवि कोडुव पावननय्या।
Hari smaraṇé maatradinta ghora duritavella naasa
Paramapurusha Purandara Vittala padavi koduva paavananayya

8. *Maraya béda*

O! Mind! Don't forget to remember Hari, the Lord!

You don't have to do yagas and yagnas
You don't have to be a Yogi or Yati

Sing and worship the Lord
who lies on the serpent and is revered by Narada!

Don't wander losing your head
thinking that your wife and sons will do you good!
When the way is lost and the time to depart comes,
Can the wife and sons come (with you)?

The moment you remember Hari,
immediately all sins are destroyed
The Supreme Person, Purandhara Vittala
gives the supreme status (liberation).

राग : पूर्वकल्याणी — Rāga : Poorvakalyāni

9. केळनो हरि-ताळनो
ताळमेळगळिद्दु प्रेमविल्लद गान (केळनो)
Kéḷanó Hari tāḷanó
tāḷaméḷagaḷiddu Premavillada gāna

तम्बूरिमुतलाद अखिल वाद्यकळिद्दु
कोम्बुकोळलुध्वनि-स्वरगळिद्दु
तुम्बुरुनारदरु गान केळुवहरि
नम्बलारइ इम्बकद कूगाडा (केळनो)
Tamboorimutalāda akhila vādyakaḷiddu
Kombukoḷaludhwani swaragaḷiddhu
tumburu Nāradaru gāna kéḷuva Hari
Nambalārai imbakada koogādā

नानाबगये राग भावकळिद्दुस्वर
ज्ञान मनो धर्म भाव इद्दु
दान वारिय दिव्य नाम रहित वाद
हीन संगीत साहित्य केमनविद्दु (केळनो)
Nānābagayé rāga bhāvakaḷiddhuswara
Jnāna manó dharma bhāva iddu
Dāna vāriya divya nāma rahita vāda
Heena sangeeta sāhitya kémanaviddu

अडिगडिगे आनन्द बाष्प पुळकदीन्द
Adigadigé ānanda bāshpa puḷakadīnda
नुडिनुडिगे श्री हरि नन्नुत
Nudi nudigé srī Hari nannuta
दृढ भक्तरु कूडि हरिकीर्तन पाडि
Dridha bhaktaru koodi Hari kīrtan paadi
कडे यल्लि पुरन्धर विटल एन्दरे केळुवा (केळनो)
Kadé yalli Purandhara vittala éndaré kéḷuvā

9. *Kélanó Hari*

Will Hari hear songs without love
even though there may be Tala and Mela (rhythm and accompaniment)?

Let there be all the musical instruments like Tambura etc.
Let there be sounds from horns and trumpets
Will Hari, who listens to the songs of Narada (who has only the Tambura), listen to the loud arrogant songs of those who do not believe in Him?

Let there by various ragas and bhavas (tunes and emotions)
and knowledge (of music), conscious will and genre,
If there is no Divine name and the lyrics and music
do not come from the heart (Will Hari hear...?)

Where at every step, tears of joy and horripilation!
Every moment, reciting the name of Sri Hari Sri Hari,
steadfast devotees assemble and sing songs of Hari,
there is present Purandhara Vittala, listening!

राग : वसंत

Rāga : Vasanta

10. "राम राम राम"

प. राम राम राम राम राम येन्निरो
सीता राम येन्निरो सीता राम येन्निरो (राम)

अ. नेमदिन्द बजिसुव वर
कामितफलव कोड्डुव नाम (राम)

P. Rāma rāma rāma rāma rāma yénniro
Sītā rāma yénniro sītā rāma yénniro (Rāma)

A. Némadinda bajisuva vara
Kāmitaphalava koḍuva nāma (Rāma)

च.1. कल्लिनन्ते इरुव जीव, निल्ल दन्ते
मरण व्याळे पुल्लनाभ कष्णनेंबो
सोल्लु बायिगे ओदगदो (राम)

C.1. Kallinanté yiruva jīva, nilla danté
maraṇa vyālé pullanābha kruṣnanémbo
Sollu bāyigé odagado (Rāma)

च.2. वातपित्त वेरड्डु कूडि श्लेष्म बन्दु
ओदगिदाग मट्टु कुंदिदाग
रघुनाथनेन्दु नेन्दु ओदगदो (राम)

C.2. Vātapitta véraḍu kūdi śléṣma bandu
Odagidāga maṭu kundidāga
Raghunāthanéndu nendu odagado (Rāma)

च.3. इहदल्लि इष्ट उण्डु परदल्लि
सुख उण्डु वर पुरन्दर विठलन्न
स्मरन बायिगे ओदगदो (राम)

C.3. Ihadalli iṣta undu paradalli
Sukha undu vara purandara viṭhalanna
Smarana bāyigé odagado (Rāma)

10. *Rama Rama Rama Rama yenniró*
Chant Rama, Rama, Rama, Rama, Rama!
Chant Sita Rama! Chant Sita Rama!

This name gives all the desired results
to those who chant it with devotion and discipline.

C.1 When the body, which is like a stone, falls
at the time of death, it may not be possible to
chant the name of Krishna!

C.2. When Vata, Pitta and Kapha combine and trouble
words become feeble,
the name of Raghunatha cannot be chanted.

C.3. Enjoying luxuries in this life,
and happiness in the other world,
It is not possible for the tongue to chant
the name of venerable Master of Purandhara.

Chant now: Rama, Rama, Rama, Rama, Rama!
Chant Sita Rama! Chant Sita Rama!

# SONGS OF SURDAS

*(15th-16th Century A.D.)*

| | *Song* | *Rāga* |
|---|---|---|
| 1. | Akhiyaan Hari darsan kee pyasee | Jogiya |
| 2. | Nisi Din barsat nain hamaare | Brindavana saranga |
| 3. | Suneri maine nirbal ke balram | Malkauns |
| 4. | Deenana Dukhaharan | Desh |
| 5. | Ham bhagatan ke bhagat | Kedar |
| 6. | Maiya moree main nahi maakhan khaayo | Bhimpalas |
| 7. | Jasoda Hari paalane jhulaawai | Misra kapi |
| 8. | Giridhar vrajadhar Murali | Durbari kanada |
| 9. | Ab main naachyo bahut Gopal | Ragesvari |
| 10. | Madhukar Syam hamaare | Bhairavi |

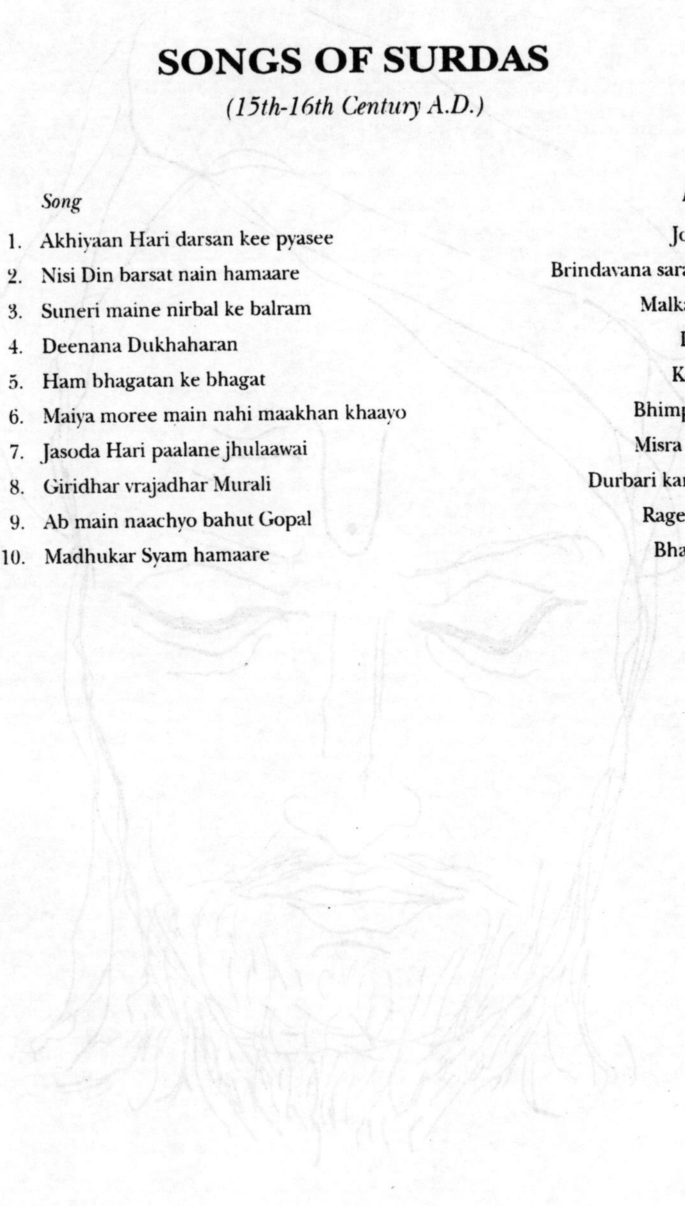

*SURDAS*

## SURDAS (1483-1563)

The blind bard, Surdas was a contemporary of Akbar. He spent most of his time singing of his beloved Krishna, somewhere between Agra and Mathura. A meeting with Saint Vallabhacharya is said to have sparked poetry about the boyhood exploits of Sri Krishna.

The main works of Surdas are: *Sursagar, Sur Saravali* and *Sahityalahari*. Surdas's songs overflow with pure, heartrending devotion.

But unlike Jayadeva and Vidyapati who deified Krishna, the Lover Surdas sang of child Krishna and his pranks. No Hindi poet has equalled Surdas in his knowledge of child psychology.

In his songs, Surdas shows his deep knowledge and understanding of the Puranas, especially the *Bhāgavata*.

To hear Surdas's songs is to transport oneself to a spiritual world brimming with love, faith and devotion.

राग : जोगिया

Rāga : Jogiya

1. अंखियाँ हरि दरसन की प्यासी
देख्यो चाहत कमल नैनको
निस दिन रहत उदासी। (अंखियाँ)
केसर तिलक की मोतियन की माला
वृन्दावन की वासी।
नेह लगाय त्यागी गये तृन सम,
डारि गये गल फाँसी। (अंखियाँ)
काहू के मनकी को जानत,
लोगन के मन हाँसी।
प्रभु सूरदास तुम्हरे दरस बिन,
लैहो करवट कासी॥ (अंखियाँ)

Aṅkhiyān hari darsan kī pyāsī
Dékhyo cāhat kamal nainako
Nis din rahat udāsī
Késar tilak kī motiyan kī mālā
Vrindāvan kī vāsī
Néha lagāy tyāgī gayé trun sam
Dāri gayé gal phaṅsī
Kāhu ké mankī ko jānat,
Logan ké man hāṅsī
Prabhu Sūrdās tumharé daras bin,
Laiho karvaṭ kāsī

1. My eyes are thirsty to have a look at Hari
I want to see the lotuseyed One
I remain sad night and day (without seeing him).
He has the saffron flower on his head and the pearl necklace.
He is the resident of Brindavan.
I have developed affection for you
and neglected my body
and put my neck in a noose,
Who knows my mind?
People laugh at me.
Lord, Surdas without seeing you,
lies, restless in Kāsi.

राग : बृन्दावन सारंग — Rāga : Brindavana-Sarang

2. निसि दिन बरसत नैन हमारे
सदा रहत पावस ऋतु हम पर
जबते स्याम सिधारे।
Nisi din barasat nain hamāré
sadā rahat pavas ritu ham par
jabté syām sidhāré
अंजन थिर न रहत अंखियन में
कर कपोल भये कारे
Anjan thir na rahat akhiyan mén
kar kapól bhayé kāré
कंचुकि पट सूखत नहि कबहूँ
उर बिच बहती पनारे।
Kancuki pat sūkhat nahi kabhun
ur bic bahati panāré
आँसू सलिल भये पग
थाके बहै जात सित तारे।
Aansoo salil bhayé pag
thāké bahain jāt sit taaré
सूरदास अब डूबत में व्रज
काहे न लेत उबारे।
Surdas ab doobat mén vraj
kaahé na lét ubāré

2. Night and day our eyes are raining (tears)
Always the season remains cloudy and thunderous
for us ever since Krishna has departed

The collyrium does not remain applied on the eyes
the hands and the cheeks have become black

The bodice is not dry since when
tears are flowing in between the breasts

The watery tears flow in countless drops
The feet have become tired

Surdas says we are in Vraj sunk
Why doesn't the Lord lift and liberate?

राग : मालकौंस

Rāga : Malkauns

3. सुने री मैंने निरबल के बलराम।

पिछली साख भरूं सन्तन की अड़े संवारे काम॥

जब लगि गाज बल अपनो बरत्यो, नेक सरयोनहिं काम

निरबल है बलराम पुकारयो, आये आधे नाम॥

द्रुपदेसुता निरबल भई ता दिन तजि आये निज धाम।

दुस्सासन की भुजा चकित भई, वसन रूप मये स्याम॥

आपबल तपबल और बाहुबल चौथी है बल दाम

सूर किशोर-कृपति सब बल, हारे को हरिनाम॥

Suné rī maiṅné nirbal ké balrām
Pichlī sākh bharūṅ santan kī adé saṅvāré kām
Jab lagi gāj bal apno baratyo, nék saryonahin kām
Nirbal hai balrām pukāryo, āyé ādhé nām
Drupad sutā nirbal bhayī, tā din taji āyé nij dhām
Dussasan kī bhujā cakit bhayī, vasan rūp mayé syām
Āpbal tapbal aur bāhubal cauthī hai bal dām
Sūr kiśor krupati sab bal, hāré ko harinām

3. O! Strong protector of the weak!
I have heard about your past reputation
in using your strength and putting things in order.
When someone called you: "Strong One! I am helpless,"
You came even before half the name was uttered
That day when Draupadi was defenceless, you came immedia-tely showing your prowess.
The hand of Dussasana got shaken, through the cloth.
O! Shyam! Self-strength, strength from penance, strength of arms all these three strengths are beaten by the fourth strength: the recital of the Lord's name!, O! Hero Krishna!

राग : देश

Rāga : Desh

4. दीनन दुख-हरन देव सन्तन, हितकारी
Deenan dukh-haran Deva santan hitakaarī
अजामील गीध व्याध, इनमें कहो कौन साध।
Ajāmīl geedh vyaadh, in mén kaho kaun saadh
पंछी को पद पढ़ात, गणिका-सी तारी॥
panchi ko pad paḍhāt, ganikāsee taaree
ध्रुव के सिर छत्र देत, प्रह्लाद को उबार लेत
Dhruv ke sir cchatr dét, Prahlād ko ubaar lét
भक्त हेत बांध्यो सेत, लंक-पुरी जारी॥
bhakt hét baandhyó sét, Lank-puree jaaree
तंदुल देत रीझ जात, साग-पातसों अघात।
tandul det reejh jāt saag-paatasón aghaat
गिनत नहिं जूठे फल, खाटे मीठे खारी।
ginat nahim jūḍhé phal, khāté meeṭé khāree
गज को जब ग्राह ग्रस्यो, दुःशासन चीर खस्यो।
gaj ko jab graah grasyo, Dussasan cheer khasyo
सभा बीच कृष्ण कृष्ण द्रौपदी पुकारी।
sabhā beech Krishn Krishn Draupadi pukaaree
इतने हरि आय गये, बसनन आरुढ़ भये
itané Hari aay gayé, basanan aaroodh bhayé
सूरदास द्वारे ठाढ़ो, आंधरो भिखारी॥
Surdās dwaaré ṭaaḍho, aandharó bhikhaaree

4. O! Lord! You remove the sorrow of the afflicted and do what benefits the good ones

Ajamila, the vulture, the hunter—Tell me who is good among these!

You made the bird fall on the way, and protected even the courtesan!

You placed the crown on Dhruva's head, and protected Prahlada

For the sake of devotees, you bridged the ocean and burnt the city of Lanka!

You were pleased with a little rice, got satiety with a meal of leaves!

You did not mind the half eaten fruit, ate the sour and sweet!

When the crocodile got hold of the elephant,

When Dussasana pulled the robe,
in the midst of the assembly, when Draupadi called: Krishna! Krishna!

Immediately You, Hari came determined to protect!

Please come to the door of Surdas, the blind beggar!

राग : केदार

Rāga : Kedar

5. हम भगतन के भगत हमारे

सुति अरजुन वरतिग्या मोरी यह बत न टारे।

भगतन काज लाजहिय धरिकै पाँय पियादे धायौ।

जहं-जहं भीर परै भगतन पै तहं-तहं होत सहायौ।

जो भगतन सो वैर करत है सो निज वरी मेरो।

देख विचार भगत-हित कारन हाँकत हौं रथ तेरौ।

जाते जीत भगत अपने की हारे हार वि चारी

सूरश्याम जो भगत विरोधी चक्र सुदरसन धारी।

Ham bhagtan ké bhagat hamāré
Suti arjun varatigyā morī yah bat na tāré
Bhagtan kāj lajhiy dhari kai pāi piyādé dhāyau
Jahaṅ jahaṅ bhīr parai bhagtan pai tahaṅ-tahaṅ hot sahāyau
Jo bhagtan so vair karat hai so nij varī méro
Dékh vicār bhagat-hit kāran hāṅkat hauṅ rath térau
Jāté jīt bhagat apné kī hāré hār vi cārī
Sūrsyām jo bhagat virodhī cakr sudarsan dhārī

5. I am the devotee of devotees!

I have heard about Arjuna's story, Don't evade me this time.

For the sake of the devotee, you gave up shame and became a footsoldier!

Wherever your devotee fell into trouble, there you came to help!

"Whoever is my devotee's enemy, he is my enemy", thinking thus, you drove the chariot for the welfare of your devotee (Arjuna).

You think that your devotee's victory is yours and devotee's defeat is your defeat!

O! Darkhued Krishna, darling of Surdas! You hold the Sudarsana disc to defeat the enemies of your devotees!

राग : भीमपलास

Rāga : Bhimpalas

6. मैया मोरी मै नहिं माखन खायो।
भोर भयो गायन के पीछे, मधुवन मोहि पठायो।
चार पहर वंशीबट भटक्यो सांझ परे घर आयो। (मैं नहीं...)
मैं बालक वहि यन को छोटो छींको किहि विधि पायो,
ग्वाल बाल सब वैर परे हैं, पर वस मुख लिपटायो। (मैं नहीं...)
तू जननी मन की अतिभोरी, इनके कहे पतियायो।
जिय तेरे कछु भेद उपजि है, जानि परायो जायो। (मैं नहीं...)
यह लै अपनी लकुट कमरिया बहुत ही नाच नचायो
सूरदास तब बिहं जसोदा, लै उर कण्ठ लगायो। (मैं नहीं...)

Maiya morī mai nahiṅ mākhan khāyo
Bhor bhayo gāyan ké pīché, madhuvan mohi paṭhāyo
Cār pahar vamśibat bhatkyo sānjh paré ghar āyo
Maiṅ bālak vahi yan ko choto chīnko kihi vidhi pāyo,
Gwāl bāl sab vair paré haiṅ, par vas mukh liptāyo
Tū jananī mankī ati bhorī, yin ké kahé patiyāyo
Jiy téré kachu bhéd upji hai, jāni parāyo jāyo
Yah lai apnī lakuṭ kamriyā bahut hī nāc nacāyo
Sūrdās tab bihaṅ jasoda, lai ur kanth lagāyo

6. "Mother mine! I did not eat butter!

It so happened that early morning, behind the singing group I was sent to Madhuvan (Sweet forest).

For twelve hours I roamed in the bamboo laden paths and returned home in the evening.

I am a small boy! How could I reach the pot of butter way above; all these youngsters are after me and have smeared the butter on my face

You, Mother are very simplehearted, you have fallen for these youngsters' accusations!

If there is even a little suspicion in your heart, I shall go elsewhere

Take this stick and blanket of yours, you have made a lot of fuss!"

Surdas sings: Yasoda then smiled and lifting him up, embraced him.

राग : मिश्रकापी

Rāga : Misrakapi

7. जसोदा हरि पालने झुलावै

हलरावै दुलराइ मल्हावै, जोइ सोई कबु गावै

मेरे लाल को आडनिदरिया, काहे न आनि सुनावै।

तू काहे नहिं बेगहिं आवै, तोकौ कान्ह बुलावै।

कबहुँ पलक हरि मुदँ लेत हैं, कबहुँ अधर फरकावै

सोवत जाति मौन है कै रहि, करि करि सैन बतावै।

इहि अंतर अकुलाय उठे हरि, जसुमत मधुरै गावै।

जो सुख 'सूर' अमर मुनि दुर्लभ, सो नंद भामिनि पावै।

Jasodā hari pālné jhulāvai
Halrāvai dulrāyi malhāvai, joyi soyī kabu gāvai
Méré lal ko āḍanidariyā, kāhé na āni sunāvai
Tū kāhé nahiṅ bégahiṅ āvai, tokau kānh bulāvai
Kabhūṅ palak hari mund lét haiṅ, kabhūṅ adhar pharkāvai
Sovat jāti maun hai kai rahi, kari kari sain batāvai
Yihi antar akulāy uṭhé hari, jasumat madhurai gavai
Jo sukh "Sūr" amar muni durlabh, so nand bhāmini pāvai

7. Yasoda, in bringing up Krishna, rocks the cradle:
Caresses him, when he tosses about, sings till he goes to sleep:

"To bring sleep to my darling son, why don't you come? O! Slumber! If you do not come quick, Krishna himself will call"

Sometimes Krishna closes his eyes, sometimes his lips keep muttering

When he goes to sleep, she keeps silent, speaks through signs,
In the meantime if Hari gets up, perturbed in mind, Yasoda sings sweetly,

That bliss, which it is difficult to attain for Surdas and other immortal angels and saints, Yasoda, wife of Nanda enjoys easily.

राग : दरबारी कानडा Rāga : Durbari Kanada

8. गिरिधर ब्रजधर मुरली अधरधर (गिरि)

Giridhar brajadhar murali adhar dhar

धरणी धर मातो पीतम्बर धर (गिरि)

Dharaṇī dhar mātó Pītāmbara dhar

शीर्शमुकुट धर गोपवेष धर (गिरि)

Sīrsamukut dhar gopavésha dhar

कर धर कमल पुष्प सारंगधर (गिरि)

Kar dhar kamal pushp sārangadhar

चक्र गदाधर अधर सुधाधर (गिरि)

Chakra gadādhar adhar sudhādhar

कम्बु कण्ठ धर कौसुभमणिधर (गिरि)

Kambukanṭa dhar Kausubhamaṇidhar

सूरदास प्रभु भक्तभार धर (गिरि)

Surdas Prabhu bhaktabhār dhar

8. He is Giridhar, the holder of the mountain, the protector of Vraja
Who holds the flute on his lips!
Mother! he is the holder of the earth and wears the yellow robe!
He wears the crown on his head and also puts on the garb of the cowherd!
He holds in his hand the lotus flower as also the bow Saranga!
He holds the discus and the mace and has nectar in his lips!
He has a neck shaped like a conch and he wears the Kaustubha gem!
The Lord of Surdas bears the burden of His devotees!

राग : रागेश्वरी

Rāga : Ragesvari

9. अब मैं नाच्यो बहुत गोपाल
काम क्रोध को पहिरि चोलना
कंठ विषयकी माल।
Ab main naachyó bahut Gopāl
kām kródhkó pahiri cholnā
kanṭh vishaykī maal
महा मोहके नूपुर बाजत
निन्दा सब्द रसाल।
mahā mohké nūpur bājat
ninda sabd rasāl
भरम भयो मन भयो पखावज
bharam bhayó man bhayó pakhaavaj
चलत कुसंगति चाल
chalat kusangati chaal
तृस्ना नाद करत घट भीतर
नाना विधि दै ताल।
trusnā nād karat ghaṭ bhītar
nānā bidhi dai tāl
माया को कटि फेटा बाँध्यो
लोभ तिलक दै भाल।
māyā kó kaṭī phéṭā bāndhyó
lobh tilak dai bhaal
कोटिक कला काछि दिखराई
जल-थल सुधि नहि काल।
koṭik kalā kaachi dikharāyi
jal-thal sudhi nahi kāl
सूरदास की सबै अविद्या
दूर करो नन्दलाल।
Surdās kī sabai avidyā
dūr karó Nandlal

9. O! Gopal! I have danced a lot
Wearing the costume of lust and anger
and the garland of the senses on the neck

The anklet of great delusion jingles and
produces the sound of spicy scandal

Suspicion and fear of the mind became the timbrel
Evil company became the gait

Desire creates noise inside the pot
and in diverse ways beats rhythm

Illusion was bound as waistband on the waist
Greed was put as tilak on the forehead

I have displayed countless tricks
and lost sense of place and time.

O! Son of Nanda! Remove all the ignorances of Surdas!

राग : भैरवी Rāga : Bhairavi

10. मधुकर स्याम हमारे चोर
मन हरि लियो माधुरी मूरति
निरख नयन की कोर।

Madhukar syām hamāré chor
man hari liyó mādhurī mūrti
nirakh nayan kī kor

पकरे हुते आन डर अन्तर
प्रेम प्रीति के जोर गये छड़ाय तोर
सब बन्धन दै गये हंसन अकोर।

pakaré huté aan dar antar
prém preeti ké jór gayé chaḍāy tór
sab bandhan dai gayé hamsan akór

उचक परों जागत निसि बीते तीरे गिनत भई भोर।
सूरदास प्रभु हरे मन मेरो सरवज लै गयो नन्दकिशोर।

uchak parón jāgat nisi beeté teeré ginat bhayī bhor
Surdas Prabhu haré man méró sarvaj lai gayo Nandkiśóre

10. Our Krishna, the dark hued Lord, full of sweetness, is a thief!
His sweet form looking through the corner of his eyes, has stolen our hearts!

He has captured the pride and fear which are inside!
His appearance has added to the pleasure of love
His stainless laughter has cut asunder all bondage!

Standing on tiptoe, awake at night, I spend on the river bank counting when it will be morning
The Lord of Surdas, Son of Nanda has stolen my heart, taken away my everything!

# SONGS OF TULSIDAS

*(16th-17th Century A.D.)*

| | *Song* | *Rāga* |
|---|---|---|
| 1. | Jaake priy na Ram Vaidehi | Hamsadhvani |
| 2. | Bhaj Raghuvar Syam jugal charan | Bahar |
| 3. | Tu dayalu | Desh |
| 4. | Raghuvar tumko meri laaj | Maru Behag |
| 5. | Nainan men Siya Ram | Lalat |
| 6. | Mamta tu na gayi | Kalavati |
| 7. | Bhaja man Ram charan | Bhairavi |
| 8. | Tumak chalat Ramachandra | Jenjoti |
| 9. | Sri Ramachandra kripalu bhaj man | Yaman |
| 10. | Janakinath sahay kare | Kalyanjenjoti |

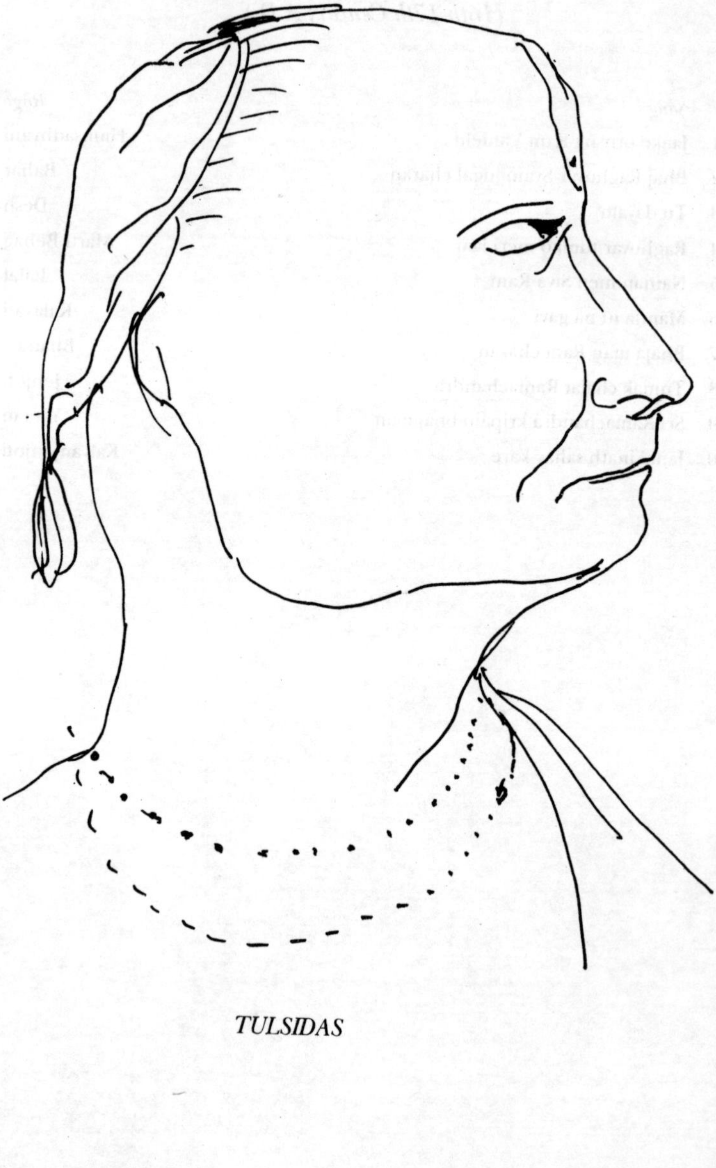

*TULSIDAS*

## TULSIDAS (1532-1623)

Details about Tulsidas's life are scanty. He was probably born in 1532 at Rajapur in Uttar Pradesh and lived most of his life—alone and unapproachable—at Varanasi, where he died in 1623. He was a contemporary of Akbar and Rana Pratap Singh of Udaipur.

Tulsidas's most famous work is the *Ramcharitmānas,* which deals with the story of Rama, Prince of Ayodhya, in loving devotion.

Tulsidas was an ardent devotee of Sri Rama as a divine incarnation of God. "The whole universe is full of Mother Sita and Lord Rama. With folded hands, I bow before them", he used to pray.

His other works include: *Krishna Gitāvali, Vinay Patrikā, Gitāvali, Kavitāvali, Dohāvali* etc. In all these works, Tulsi's devotion to God is explicit.

Tulsidas wrote his poetry in *Lok Bhasha* and *Braj Bhasha,* two dialects of Hindi.

The songs of Tulsidas, selected for this book, represent a sampling of his devotional lyrics.

राग : हंसध्वनि

Rāga : Hamsadhvani

1. जाके प्रिय न राम वैदेही।

Jaaké priy na Ram vaidéhī

सो छाँड़िये कोटि बैरी सम,

जद्यपि परम सनेही॥

So cchādiyé koti bairee sam

Jadyapi param snéhī

तज्यो पिता प्रह्लाद, विभीषण बन्धु,

भरत महतारी।

Tajyó pitā Prahlād, Vibheeshaṇ bandhu

Bharat mahatāree

बलि गुरु तज्यो, कंत ब्रजबनितनि,

भये मुद-मंगलकारी॥

Bali guru tajyo, Kant vrajabanitani

Bhayé muda mangalakaaree

नाते नेह राम के मनियत

सुहृद सुसेव्य जहाँ लौं।

Nāté néh Rām ké maniyat

suhrud susévya jahān laun

अंजन कहा आँखि जेहि फूटै,

बहु तक कहौं कहाँ लौं

Anjan kahā aankhi jéhi phootai

Bahu tak kahaun kahān laun

तुलसी सो सब भाँति

परमहित पूज्यप्रान ते प्यारो

Tulsī so sab bhānti

Paramhit poojya prān té pyāro

जासों होय सनेह रामपद,

एतो मतो हमारो॥

Jaason hoi sneh Rampad

étó mató hamāró

1. Those to whom Rama and Sita are not dear

should be given up like bitterest enemies even if they are intimate friends.

Prahlada gave up his father, Vibhishana his relatives, Bharata his mother.

Bali gave up his teacher, Krishna the young women of Vraja. Everything turned out to be auspicious and good at the end.

Relationship with Rama should be deemed respectful and loving, overriding other relationships.

How can you say that the collyrium will ever hurt the eyes?

To Tulsi, Rama appears supremely pleasing and venerable and dearer than lifebreath.

Whosoever has love towards the feet of Rama (is dearer than lifebreath).
This is our belief.

राग : बहार

Rāga : Bahār

2. भज रघुवीर श्याम जुगलचरण

Bhaj Raghuvīr syām jugalcharan

इत ही अयोध्या निर्मल शरयू

Ita hī Ayodhyā nirmal sarayū

उत गोकुल जमुना (भज)

Uta Gokul Jamunā

इत पाही पर सिय विराजे

Ita paahī par siya virājé

उत राधा संग रमण (भज)

Uta Radha sang raman

इत तुलसी उत सूरविराजे,

Ita Tulsi uta sūr virājé

जुगल चरण जित धरणा (भज)

Jugal charan jit dharanā

2. Worship the feet of Rama and Krishna

Here is Ayodhya and the pure Sarayu river

There it is Gokul and the Yamuna river

Here shines Sita on the lap

There it is sporting with Radha

Here is Tulsi, there is Surdas

Who meditate on the two pairs of feet.

राग : देश

Rāga: Desh

3. तू दयालु, दीन हौं, तू दानि, हौं भिखारी।
हौं प्रसिद्ध पातकी, तू पाप-पुंज-हारी॥
नाथ तू अनाथ को, अनाथ कौन मोसो।
मो समान आरत नहिं आरतिहर तोसो॥
ब्रह्म तू, हौं जीव, तू है ठाकुर, हौं चेरो।
तात-मातु, गुरु-सखा, तू सब बिधि हितु मेरो॥
तोहिं मोहिं नाते अनेक, मानियै जो भावै।
ज्यों त्यों तुलसी कृपालु! चरन सरन पावै॥
हे नाथ! तू दीनों पर दया करने वाला है तो मैं दीन हूं।

Tū dayālu, dīn hauṁ, tū dāni, hauṁ bhikhārī
Hauṁ prasidh pātakī, tū pāp-punj-hāri
Nāth tū anāth ko, anāth kaun moso
Mo samān ārat nahiṁ āratihar toso
Brahm tū, hauṁ jīv, tū hai ṭhākur, hauṁ cero
Tāt-mātu, guru-sakhā tū sab bidhi hitu méro
Tohiṁ mohiṁ nāte anek, māniyai jo bhāvai
Jyoṁ tyoṁ tulsi krupālu! caran saran pāvai
He nāth! tū dīnoṁ par dayā karné vālā hai to maiṁ dīn huṁ

3. You are kind, I am the pitiable one,
You are the donor, I am the beggar,
I am the notorious sinner, You are the destroyer of accumulated sins,
You are master, I am the orphan, who is orphaned like me?
There is no one afflicted like me, and no one to destroy affliction like you,
You are the Supreme Self, I am the individual soul,
You are the Zamindar, I am the servant,
Father, Mother, Teacher, Friend, you are my helper in all ways.
Between you and me there are so many relationships.
whatever Tulsi feels that you are,
O! Compassionate One! I seek refuge in your feet,
O! Lord! If you are the One who shows mercy on the poor, then I am the poor one.

राग : मरु बेहाग

Rāga : Maru behāg

4. रघुवर तुम को मेरी लाज।

Raghuvar tum kó méri laaj

सदा सदा मैं सरण तिहारी
तुमहि गरीब निवाज।

Sadā sadā mai saran tihārī
tumhi gareeb nivāj

पतित उधारन विरद तुम्हारो,
स्रवनन सुनी आवाज।

Patit udhāran virad tumhāró
sravavan sunee aavaaj

हौं तो पतित पुरातन कहिये,
पार उतारो जहाज।

Haum tó patit purātana kahiyé
pār utāró jahāj

अघ-खंडन दुख भंजन
जन के यही तिहारो काज।

Agha khanḍan dukh bhanjan
jan ke yahee tihāró kaaj

तुलसी दास पर किरपा कीजै,
भगति दान देहु आज।

Tulsidas par kripā keejai
Bhagati dān dehu aaj

4. O! Rama, Scion of Raghus! To you, my sense of shame!
Always I seek refuge in you
You have to be in this poor one's residence

Your vow is to uplift the fallen
Let your ears hear my voice!

I am a fallen one since long
Make this boat cross across!

Destroying sin and sorrow of people
This is your job!

Please have mercy on Tulsidas
Give me devotion (to you) today!

राग : ललत

Rāga : Lalat

5. नैनन में सियाराम
बसोजी मेरे
जनक नन्दिनी जगदवन्दिनी
रघुनायक घनश्याम (नैनन)
कनक मण्डप तले रत्नसिंहासन
जुगल मूर्ति अभिराम (नैनन)
सरयू तीरे अयोध्यानगरी
चित्रकूट निजधाम
तुलसीदास प्रभु की छवि निरकत
लजत कोटि शतकाम (नैनन)

Nainan mén Siyā Rām
Basojī méré
Janak nandini jagatvandinī
Raghunāyak ghansyām
Kanak mandap talé ratnasinhāsan
Jugal mūrti abhirām
Sarayoo teeré Ayodhyānagarī
Chitrakoot Nij dhām
Tulsidas Prabhu kī cchavi nirkat
Lajat kóti satkām

5. Let Sita and Ram reside in my eyes
the daughter of Janaka, venerated in the universe
and the scion of Raghus who is darkhued like the clouds
Let Sita and Ram reside in my eyes!
In the golden mandap, on the diamondstudded throne the beautiful pair
The city of Ayodhya on the banks of the Sarayu river (is the capital),
but the real residence is Chitrakoot

The radiant beauty of Tulsidas's Lord
shames a hundred million Cupids!

राग : कलावती Rāga : Kalāvatī

6. ममता तू न गई मेरे मन ते
पाके कैस जनम के साथी
लाज गई लोकन ते।
Mamta tū na gaī méré man té
Pāké kais janam ké saathī
lāj gaī lokan té
तन थाके कर काँपन लागे
ज्योति गई नैनन ते।
Tan thāké kar kāmpan laagé
Jyoti gaī nainan té
सखन वचन न सुनत काहु के
बल गये सब इंद्रिन ते।
Sakhan vachan na sunat kāhoo ké
bal gayé sab indrin té
टूटे दसन वचन नहिं आवत,
सोभा गई मुखन ते,
Tooté dasan vachan nahim aavat
sobhā gaī mukhan té
कफ पित बात कंठ पर बैठ,
सुतहि बुलावत कर ते।
Kaph pit bāt kanṭ par baiṭ
Sutahim bulāvat kar té
भाई बंधु सब परम पियारे
नारि निकारत घर ते।
Bhāī bandhu sab param pyāré
Nāri nikārat ghar té
जैसे ससि मंडल बिच स्याही
छुटै न कोटि जनन ते।
Jaisé sasi mandal bich syāhī
Chutai na koti janan té
तुलसीदास बलि जाऊँ
चरन ते लोभ पराये धन ते॥
Tulsidas bali jāoon
Charan té lobh parāé dhan té

6. Pride! You have not yet left my mind!
Having got such a lifelong companion
I am ashamed to look at myself.

The body remains, but the hands have begun to shake
Light has gone away from the eyes!

I am not able to hear every word of anyone's speech
Strength has gone from all sensory organs!

Teeth are broken, speech does not come
radiance has gone from the face!

Phlegm,bile and rheumatism are sitting around the neck
Even the son calls by show of hands

All dear ones: brothers, relatives and wife kick me out of the house

Like the black stain on the moon
even with a million births, there is no liberation!

Tulsidas wants to offer at your feet
as a sacrificial offering: greed for other people's money!

राग : भैरवी Rāga : Bhairavi

7. भज मन राम चरन सुख दाई

जिहि चरननि से निकसी सुरसरि संकर जटा समाई

जटा संकरी नाम पर्‌यो है, त्रिभुवन तारन आई।

Bhaj man Rām charan sukhadāee

Jihi charanani sé nikasī surasari sankar jatā samāee

Jatā sankaree nām paryó hai, tribhuvan tāran aayee

जिन चरनन की चरन पादुका भरत रह्यो लव लाई

Jin charanan kī charan pādukā Bharat rahyó lav lāee

साइ चरन केवट धोइ लीने तब हरि नाव चलाई।

Sāi charan kévat dhoi leené tab Hari nāv chalāee

सोई चरन गौतम-ऋषि-नारी परसि परम पद पाई।

Soī charan Gautam rishi nāree parasi param pad pāee

दंडक वन प्रभु पावन कीन्हा ऋषियन त्रास मिटाई।

Dandak van Prabhu pāvan kīnhā rishiyan trās miṭāee

सोई प्रभु त्रिलोक के स्वामी कनक मृगा संग धाई

Soī Prabhu trilok ké swāmī kanak mrigā sang dhāī

कपि सुग्रीव बधु भय-व्याकुल तिन जय छत्र फिरि।

Kapi sugreeva badhu bhay vyākula tin jay cchatr phiri

रिपु का अनुज विभीषन निसिचर परसत लंका पाई।

Ripu kā anuj Vibheeshan nisichar parasat lankā pāee

सिव सनकादिक अरु ब्रह्मादिक शेष सहस मुख गाई।

Siva Sanakādik aru Brahmādika sésh sahas mukh gāee

तुलसी दास मारुत सुत का प्रभु निज मुख करत बड़ाइ।

Tulsidās Mārutsut kā Prabhu nij mukh karat baḍāi

7. O! Mind! worship the feet of Rama, which give happiness!
From which feet, the heavenly river started and was held by Sankara's matted hair
Sankara's matted hair has since become famous as the saviour of the three worlds!

The sandals of which feet, Bharata kept and Lava brought
The same feet the boatman (Guha) washed and then plied the boat for the Lord!

The same feet the wife of sage Gautama touched
and attained the supreme status!

With the same feet, the Lord made the forest of Dandaka pure and protected the sages therein

The same Lord, who is Master of the three worlds
ran after the golden deer!

Monkey Sugriva's wife was afflicted with fear
Victory there opened the royal umbrella (for Sugriva)!

Demon Enemy's younger brother, Vibhishana touched (those feet) and attained the kingdom of Lanka!

Siva, Sanaka, Brahma and thousands others sang of his glory.

And the Lord of Tulsidas and Hanuman (the son of wind) appeared and blessed.

राग : जेंजोटी Rāga : Jenjoti

8. ठुमक चलत रामचन्द्र बाजत पैजनियाँ
किलकि किलकि उठत धाय गिरत भूमि लटपटाय
धाई मात गोद लेत दशरथ की रानियाँ
विद्रुम से अेरुण अधर बोलत मुख मधुर मधुर
शुभग नासिका में चारु लटकटलत कनियाँ
तुलसीदास अति आनंद देख के मुखारविन्द
रघुवर छवि की समान रघुवर छवि वाणियाँ ॥

Ṭumak chalat Ramachandr baajat paijaniyaan
Kilaki kilaki uṭat dhāy gīrat bhoomi latpatāy
Dhāi māt gód lét dasarath kī rāniyān
Vidrum sé arun adhar bólat mukh madhur madhur
Subhag nāsikā mén charū latkatlat kaniyān
Tulsidas ati ānand dekh ké mukhāravind
Raghuvar cchavi kī samān Raghuvar cchavi vaaniyaan

8. Gracefully walks Ramachandra and the anklets jingle!
Joyously gets up and runs and falls on the ground stumbling!
The mother runs and takes him on the lap, the pride of Dasaratha!
The lips which are more red than coral speak sweet words
On the auspicious nose, hang beautiful diamonds
Tulsidas is very happy seeing the lotusface
The beauty of Ram is equalled only by the beauty of his lispings!

राग : यमन

Raga : Yaman

9. श्रीरामचन्द्र कृपालु भजु मन हरण भवभय दारुणं।
नवकंज-लोचन, कंज-मुख, कर-कंज, पद कंजारुणं॥
कंदर्प अगणित अमित छबि, नवनील नीरद सुंदरं।
पटपीत मानहुं तड़ित रुचि शुचि नौमि जनक सुतावरं॥
भजु दीनबंधु दिनेश दानव-दैत्यवंश-निकंदनं।
रघुनंद आनंदकंद कोसलचंद दशरथ-नंदनं॥
सिर मुकुट कुंडल तिलक चारु उदारु अंग विभूषणं।
आजानुभुज शर-चाप-धर, संग्राम-जित-खरदूषणं॥
इति बदति तुलसीदास शंकर-शेष-मुनि-मन-रंजनं।
मम हृदय कंज निवास कुरु, कामादि खल-दल-गंजनं॥

Śrīrāṁacandra krupālu bhaju man haran bhav bhay dāruṇaṁ
Navkanj-locan, kanj-mukh, kar̃-kanj, pad kanjāruṇaṁ
Kandarp agaṇit amit cchabi, navnīl nīrad sundaraṁ
Patpīt mānahuṁ taḍit ruci śuci naumi janak sutā varaṁ
Bhaju dīnabandhu dineś dānav-daitya vaṁś-nikandanaṁ
Raghunand ānandkand kosalacand dasarath-nandanaṁ
Sir mukuṭ kundal tilak caru udāru ang vibhūṣaṇaṁ
Ājānubhuj śar cāp dhar, sangrām jit-kharadūṣaṇaṁ
Iti badati tulsidas śankar-śeṣ-muni-man ranjanaṁ
Mama hruday kanj nivās kuru, kāmādi khal-dal-ganjanaṁ

9. O! Mind! Worship the compassionate Sri Ramachandra,
who destroys the pitiable fear of the phenomenal world.
His eyes are like fresh lotuses, He is lotus-faced,
His hands are like lotuses, his feet are crimson like lotuses.
His beauty excels that of myriad Cupids, He is handsomely blue hued like the cloud,
I bow before the One who wed the daughter of Janaka,
who wears the yellow garment, the pure One who destroys arrogance.
Worship the friend of the poor, the Sun who destroys the families of demons.
The progeny of Raghu, the son of Dasaratha, the reservoir of bliss, the moon to Kosala,
Worship the one who wears the crown on his head,
ear ornaments and the crimson mark on the forehead,
whose every limb is decorated beautifully and generously,
who has a tall stature, wellbuilt with strong arms,
carrying the bow and arrows, and is victorious over evil demons in battle,
Thus says Tulsidas, worship Him, who pleases Sankara and all the sages,
Reside in the lotus of my heart, destroying evil feelings like lust.

राग : कल्याण जेंजोटी Rāga : Kalyanjenjoti

10. जानकीनाथ सहाय करे जब
कौन बिगाड़ करे नर तेरो (जानकी नाथ)

Jānakīnath sahāy karé jab
Kaun bigāḍ karé nar téró

सूरज मंगल सोम भृगुसुत।
बुध अरु गुरु वरदायक तेरो।

Sūraj mangal som bhrigusut
Budh aru guru varadāyak téró

राहु केतु की नाहि गम्यता
संग शनीचर होत उचेरो।

Rāhu kétu kī nāhi gamyatā
Sang sanīchar hot uchéró

दुष्ट दुःशासन विमल द्रौपदी
चीर उतार कुमन्तर प्रेरो

Dust Dussasan vimal Draupadī
Cheer utār kumantar préró

जाकी सहाय करी करुणानिधि
बढ़ गये चीर के मार घनेरी

Jākī sahāy karī karunānidhi
Baḍ gayé cheer ké mār ghanérī

गरभ में राख्यो परीक्षित राजा
अश्वत्थामा जब अस्त्र प्रेरो
भारत में मरुही के अंडा
ता पर गजका घंटा गेरो॥

Garbh mén rākhyó Pareekshit Rājā
Aswatthāmā jab astr préró
Bhārat mén maruhī ké andā
Tā par gajkā ghantā géró

जाकि सहाय करी करुणानिधि
ताके जगत में भाग बड़ेरो
रघुवंशी संतन सुखदायी
तुलसीदास चरणन को चेरो॥

Jāki sahāy karī Karunānidhi
Tāké jagat mén bhāg badhéró
Raghuvamsee santan sukhadāyī
Tulsidās charaṇan kó chéro

10. When Rama, the Lord of Janaki, helps you
O! Man! who can mess up your affairs?

The sun, Mars, moon and Venus
Mercury and Jupiter will confer boons on you

Rahu and Ketu will not approach you
Along with Saturn they will be favourable to you

Evil Dussasan prodded by evil designs, removed the robe of
Stainless Draupadi

The Ocean of mercy went and helped
and the cloth went on lengthening and became a heavy pile!

King Pareekshit was protected in the womb,
When Aswatthama sent the arrow
In Mahabharata,
So was the egg of the tiny insect (ant) protected when the bell
of the elephant fell on it.

The Ocean of mercy went and helped
so that in the universe goodness may increase
Rama, the progeny of the family of Raghus, gives happiness,
Tulsidas is the servant of his feet.

# SONGS OF TUKARAM

*(17th Century A.D.)*

| | *Song* | *Rāga* |
|---|---|---|
| 1. | Tu majha maay baap | Behag |
| 2. | Sundar te dhyaan | Desh |
| 3. | Aajee anandu re | Tilang |
| 4. | Dhanya te Pandari | Sarang |
| 5. | Sadaa maajhe dola | Kalingda |
| 6. | Baa re Panduranga | Yaman |
| 7. | Aanik dusere | Bhaagya Sree |
| 8. | Naam ghetaam uta uti | Dhanee |
| 9. | Anandacha Kand | Bhimpalas |
| 10. | Pandari Pandari | Asaveri |

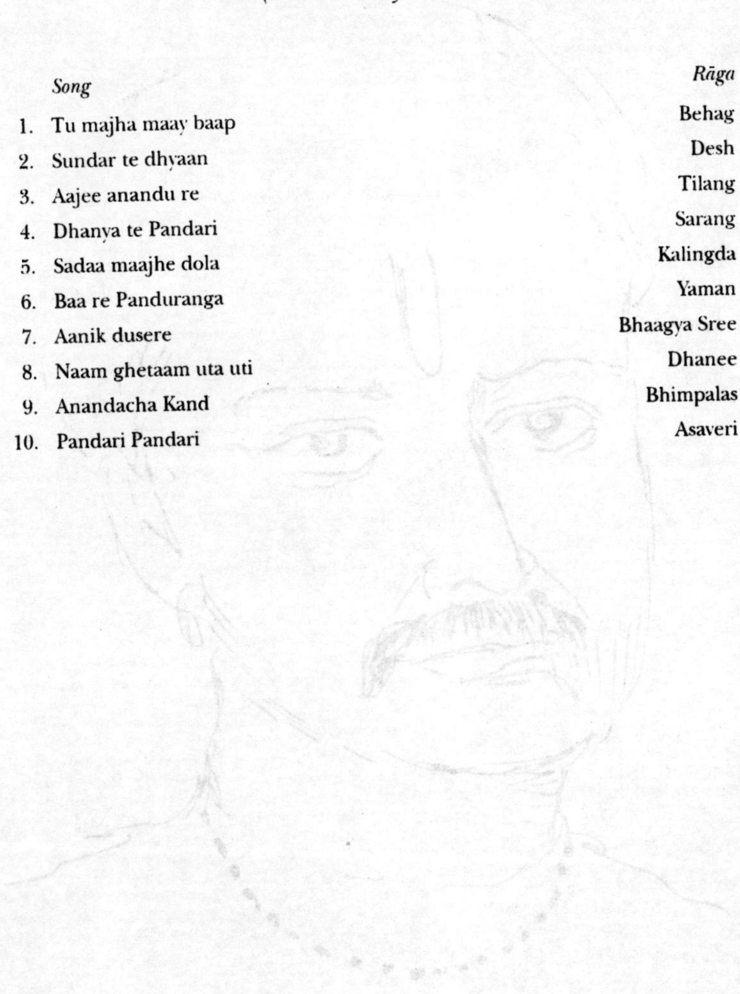

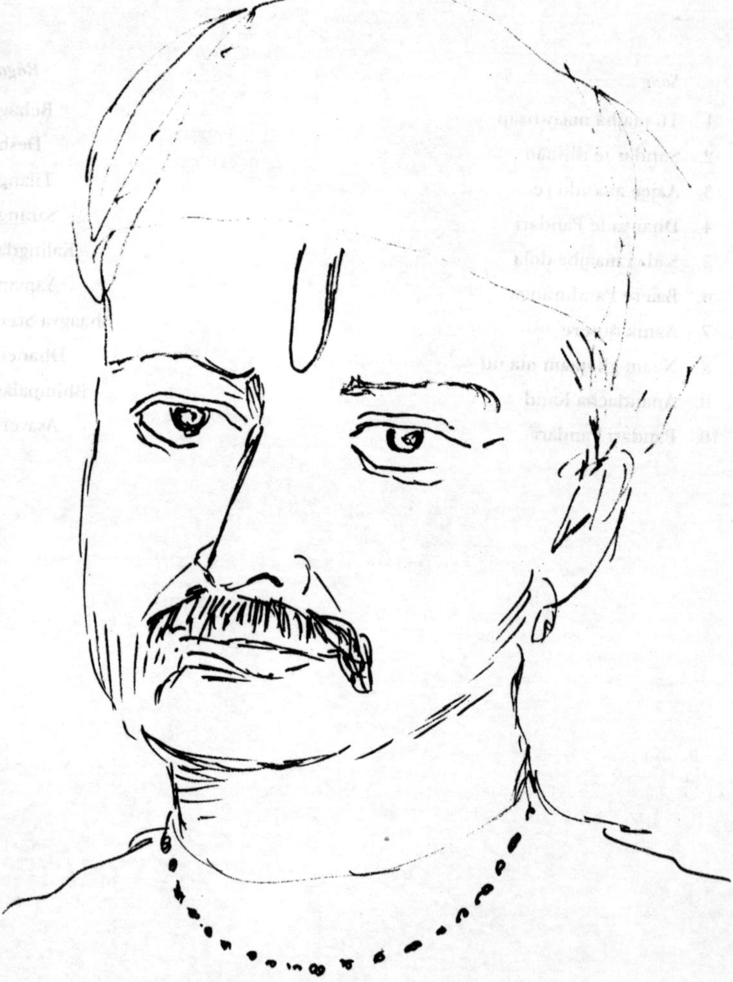

*TUKARAM*

# TUKARAM (1608-1650)

Saint Tukaram was born in a small village named Dehu in Maharashtra in the year 1608. Like his parents, he was a devotee of Vitthal of the temple at Pandharpur.

In his life, Tukaram underwent a lot of misery, including extreme poverty. His family business ran into losses, his first wife died and his second wife, Jijabai, proved to be a shrew. But Tukaram remained unflinching in his devotion to the Lord of Pandharpur and composed mellifluous songs to His Divine Master.

Tukaram's songs are known as *Abhangs* (meaning: unbreakable ones).

What he sang was dutifully recorded by two of his disciples: Gangaram Maval and Santaji Teli and transferred to posterity. Today they are a part of the psyche of the people of Maharashtra.

Tukaram was a contemporary of Shivaji, who was one of his admirers.

Tukaram conducted prayer meetings, singing bhajans, to which a large number of people flocked and his fame spread.

He died in 1650.

As one of his disciples declared: No one could match Tukaram in *Jnāna, Bhakti* and *Vairāgya* (knowledge, devotion and detachment).

His songs display rustic simplicity, deep devotion and a frank intimacy with his beloved personal God: Vitthala of Pandharpur.

राग : बेहाग

Rāga : Béhāg

1. तूं माझा माय बाप सकल वित्तगोत
तूंचि माझे हित कर्ता देवा
तूंचि माझा देव तूंचि माझा जीव
तूंचि माझा भाव पांडुरंगा।
तूंचि माझा आचार तूं माझा विचार
तूंचि सर्व भार चालविसी
सर्व भावें मज तूं होसी प्रमाण
ऐसी तुझी आण वाहत सें
तुका म्हणे तुज विकला जीव भाव
कळेल तो उपाय करो आतां।

Tūṅ mājhā māy bāp sakal vittagot
Tūṅci mājhé hit kartā dévā
Tūṅci mājhā dév tūṅci mājhā jīv
Tūṅci mājhā bhāv pāṇḍurangā
Tūṅci mājhā ācār tūṅ mājhā vicār
Tuṅci sarv bhār cālvisī
Sarv bhāvéṅ maj tūṅ hosī pramāṇ
Aisī tujhī āṇ vāhat séṅ
Tukā mhaṇé tuj viklā jīv bhāv
Kaḷél to upāy karo ātāṅ

1. *Tu mājhā māy baap*

You are my mother, father, riches, relatives, my all.
O! God! You alone can do what is good for me.
You are my God, my life!
You are my feeling, O! Panduranga!
You are my action, my thought.
You help bear all my burdens.
You are the basis of all my emotions.
This I solemnly affirm.
Tuka says: "I have sold my life and thought to you,
use such means (to help me) as you deem fit."

राग : देश Rāga : Desh

2. सुन्दर ते ध्यान उभे विटेवरी
करकटीवरी ठेवुनिया
मकरकुण्डल तलपती श्रवणी
कण्ठी कौस्तुभ मणी विराजित
गला तुलसी हार कासे पीताम्बर
आवडे निरन्तर हेचि ध्यान
तुकाह्मणे माझे हेचि सर्वसुख
पाहि न श्री मुख आवडीने
कृष्ण राम हरि मुकुन्द मुरारी
अच्युत नर हरि नारायण॥

Sundar té dhyān ubhé vitévarī
karakaṭī varī ṭévuniyā
makar kundala talapatī śravaṇī
kanṭhi koustubha manī virājita
Galā tulasī hār kāsé pītāmbar
āvaté nirantar héci dhyān
Tukāhmaṇé mājhé héci sarvasukh
Pāhi na śrī mukh āvadīné
kruṣṇa rām hari mukund murāri
Accut narhari nārāyaṇ

2. *Sundar té dhyān*

Beautiful is your form standing on the brick
keeping your hands on the waist,
Crocodile-shaped ear-rings are shining on your ears!
The Kaustubha gem is radiant on your neck!
So too is the Tulsi garland! And the yellow silk robe!
I always love this form
Says Tukaram, this is my entire happiness
I shall ever see the Lord's face with pleasure.
O! Krishna! O! Rama! O! Hari! O! Mukunda! O! Murari!
O! Achyuta! O! Narahari! O! Narayana!

राग : तिलंग Rāga : Tilang

3. आजी आनन्दु रे एकी परमानन्दु रे
जया स्त्रुति नेति नेति म्हणती गोन्दिुरे
विठोबासी भेटी आम्हा आनन्दु सदा
गावूँ नाचूँ वावूँटाली रिजवूँ गोविन्दा
सदासण सन्ता आम्हा नित्य दीवाली
आनन्द निर्भर आमुचा कैवारी भाळी
तुकाह्मणे नाही जन्म मरणाचा धाक
सन्त सनकादिक ते आमुचे कौतुक ॥

Ājī ānandu ré ékī paramānandu ré
jayā sruti néti neti mhaṇatī Govinduré
Vitobāsibhéti āmha ānandu sadā
Gāvoon nāchoon vavoontalī rijvu Govinda
Sadāsaṇ santā āmha nitya Dīwālī
Ananda nirbhar āmucha kaivāri paḷi
Tukāhmané nāhi janmamaranācha tāk
Sant sanakādik té amuché kautuk

3. *Aajee ānandu ré*

Today is a day of bliss, supreme bliss
When we recite the names of Govinda, the joy is incomparable!
Visiting Vithoba is always bliss for us.
We sing, dance and clap our hands to entertain Govinda!
For us, devotees, everyday is Diwali!
Our joy is fearless, for the Lord protects us!
Tukaram says: "Let there be no fear of birth and death!"
Being with the Lord is the permanent desire of all devotees (like Sanaka).

राग : सारंग

Rāga : Sarang

4. धन्यते पण्ठरी धन्य भीमातीर
आणिचेले सार पुण्डलीक
धन्यते हि लोक, अवधा दैवोत्सव
सकल प्रेमोत्सव धरोधरी
धन्यते हि भूमी धन्य तरुवर
धन्यते सरोवर तीर्थ रूप
धन्यते नर नारी मुखी नाम ध्यान
आनन्द भुवन गर्ज ताती
धन्यते पशु पक्षी कीटक पाषाण
अवधा नारायण अवतर लासे
तुकाह्मणे धन्य संसाराते आळि
हरी रंगी रंगली सर्वभाव।

Dhanyaté paṇḍarī dhany bhīmātīr
Ānicélé sār pundalīk
dhanyaté hi lok avadhā daivotsav
sakāl prémótsav dharodharī
dhanyaté hi bhūmi dhany taruvar
dhanyaté sarovar tīrth rūp
dhanyaté narnārī mukhī nām dhyān
ānand bhuvan garj tātī
dhanyaté pasu pakṣī kītak pāṣāṇ
avadhā nārāyaṇ avtar lāsé
tukāhmaṇé dhany samsārāté āḷi
Harī rangī ranglī sarv bhāv

4. *Dhanya té Panḍari*

Blessed is this city of Pandharpur, blessed is the river bank of Bhima!

Pundalik (the devotee) has brought the essence (of life) here!

Blessed are the people here to enjoy the grace of the Lord!

His bounty of love is seen in every house

Blessed is this land, blessed the trees!

The water of this lake is like holy nectar!

Blessed are these men and women, who chant the Lord's name and sing His praises,

The happy homes are filled with the echo of their music,

Blessed are the animals, birds, insects and stones of this place as Narayana has appeared in this city!

Tukaram says: all are blessed here,

despite household and family duties, everyone's feelings and emotions are focussed on Lord Hari!

राग : कलिंगडा

Rāga : Kalingda

5. सदा माझे डोलां जडो तुझी मूर्ति।

रखुमाईच्या पति सोयरिया॥

sadā mājhé dolā jadó tujhī mūrti
rakhumaīchyā pati sóyariyā

गोड तुझें रूप गोड तुझें नाम।

देई मज प्रेम सर्व काल॥

góda tujhén roopa goda tujhén nām
deī maja prem sarva kāl

विठो माउलिये हाचि वर देई।

संचरोनी राही हृदयामाजी॥

vitho maoliyé hāchi vara déī
sancharónī rāhī hridayāmājee

तुका म्हणे कांही न मांगे आणीक।

तुझे पायी सुख सर्व आहे॥

Tuka mhaṇé kāhi na mangé aanīk
tujhé pāyee sukh sarv aahé

5. *Sadaa maajhé dolā*

O! Lord! Let your image be in my eyes always!
You are the husband of Rukmini, but you are our relative as well!

Sweet is your form, sweet is your name!
Give me love for you for all times!

O! Mother Vithal! grant me a boon
that you will always be in my heart!

Tukaram says: I do not ask for anything else!
All my happiness is being at your feet (O! Lord!)

राग : यमन Rāga : Yaman

6. बा रे पांडुरंगा केव्हां येसी भेटी
जाहालों हिंपुटी तुंजवीण ॥
Bā ré Panduraṅgā kévhān yésī bhétī
jāhālon himputī tujaveeṇa
तुजवीण सखें नाहीं मज कोणी
वाटतें चरणीं घालूं मिठी ॥
tujveena sakhé nāhīn maja kóṇī
vātaté charaṇeem ghāloon mithī
ओंवाळावी काया चरणावरोनी
केव्हा चक्रपाणी भेट शील ॥
Omvāḷāvī kāyā charanāvarónee
kevhā chakrapāni bhét śeel
तुका म्हणे माझी पुरवी आवडी।
वेगें घालीं उडी नारायणा ॥
Tuka mhaṇé mājhī puravī aavadī
végén ghālī udī Nārāyaṇā

6. *Baa ré Pānduranga*

O! Panduranga! When will you come to meet me?
I am sad and lost without you!

I have no friend except you
I am longing to prostrate before you and embrace your feet!

I want to throw my body at your feet
O! Lord who hold the discus in your hand! When will you meet me?

Tukaram says: "Please fulfil my wish and come at once to meet me, O! Narayana! Abode of all beings!

राग : भाग्यश्री Rāga : Bhāgyasree

7. आणिक दुसरे मज नाही आता।
नेमिलें या चित्तापासुनियां॥

Āṇik dusaré maj nāhi aata
némilé yā chittāpāsuniyān

पांडुरंग ध्यानीं पांडुरंग मनीं।
जागृती स्वप्नीं पांडुरंग॥

Pandurang dhyānīm Pandurang manīm
jāgriti swapnīm Pāndurang

पडिलें वळण इंद्रियां सकलां।
भाव तो निराळा नाहीं दुजा॥

padilém vaḷaṇ indriyān sakalām
bhāv tó nirāḷā nāhim dujā

तुका म्हणे नेत्रीं केली ओळखण।
तटस्थ ते ध्यान विटेवरी॥

Tuka mhaṇé nétrim kélī oḷakhaṇ
tatastha té dhyān vitévarī

7. *Aanik dusaré*

I have nothing else in my mind except
this thought (of the Lord)

Pandurang is in my thought, Pandurang is in my mind!
In my waking state and in my sleep and dreams, I think of Pandurang!

All my senses are tuned to this thought
and there is no other feeling whatsoever!

Tukaram says: "My eyes only notice the quiet image (of the Lord) standing on the brick."

राग : धनी

Rāga : Dhanee

8. नाम घेतां उठा उठी ।
होय संसाराची तुटी ॥
nām ghetām uṭauṭī
hoy samsārāchī tutī
ऐसा लाभ बांधा गांठी ।
विठ्ठल पायीं पडे मिठी ॥
aisā lābh bāndhā gānṭī
Viṭṭal pāyeem padé miṭī
नामापरतें साधन नाहीं ।
जो तूं करिसी आणिक कांही ॥
nāmāparatém sādhan nāhīm
jo tū karisī ānik kāhī
हां कारोनी सांगे तुका ।
नाम धेतां राहो नका ॥
hān kārónī sāngé Tuka
nām dhétā rāhó nakā

8. *Naam ghétaam uta uti*

Sing the name of the Lord all the time
(Not to sing) is the shortcoming of Samsara

Collect the goodwill in such a way
that you will (finally) rest at Lord Vittal's feet!

There is no other way than chanting the Lord's name
This is easy and can be done, while you are doing your daily chores.

Tukaram entreats you all: "Please do not forget to chant the Lord's name!"

राग : भीमपलास Rāga : Bhimpalas

9. आनंदाचा कंद हरि हा।
Ānandāchā kand Hari hā
देवकी नंदन पाहिला।
Devakī nandan pāhilā
भक्तासाठीं ठेउन कर कटीं
भीमानिकटीं राहिला।
Bhaktāsāṭī téun kar katīm
Bhīmanikatim rāhilā
कंसभयानें वसुदेवानें
नंद यशोदे वाहिला।
Kamsa bhayāné Vasudévāném
Nanda yaśodé vāhilā
यज्ञयाग जपतपासी न भुले,
ध्यान धारणे नाकळे।
Yagna yāga japatapāsī na bhulé
dhyāna dhārané nākaḷé
निश्चय साचा परि तुकयाचा
भक्तिगुणासी मोहिला
Nischay sāchā paṛi Tukayāchā
Bhaktiguṇāsī móhilā

9. *Ānandāchā kand*

The root of happiness is this Hari
the son of Devaki whom I saw.

He is standing, with his arms resting on the waist
and waiting for his devotees, on the Bheema river bank!

Fearing Kamsa, Vasudeva
gave away his son to Nandagopa and Yasoda

Tukaram is not enamoured of rituals like Yagna, yaga, mechanical repetition, penance or meditation and concentration

Tukaram is determined to pray to the Lord
with love, faith and devotion.

राग : असावेरी Rāga : Asaveri

10. पंढरी पंढरी विठरायाची नगरी
Panḍari Panḍari Viṭarāyāchee nagarī
भंवता भिवरेचा वेढा
bhavatā bhivaréchā veḍā
मध्ये पंढरीचा हुडा।
madhyé Panḍareechā hudā
गस्त फिरे चहंकोनीं
gasta phiré chahankoneem
ढाळ मृदंगाची ध्वनी
ḍāḷa mridangāchī dhvanī
ऐसे स्थल आहे कोठें
aisé sthal aahé koṭém
तुकयाला विठ्ठल भेटे॥
Tukayālā Viṭṭal bhété

10. *Panḍari Panḍari*

Pandharpur is the great city of Lord Vittala

This city is surrounded by the crescent of river Bheema

In the centre, rests the treasure of Pandharpur: Panduranga!

Devotees (security guards) walk on all four sides

The sound of drums and bells echoes everywhere!

Can you ever find such a place anywhere (in the world)?

Tukaram meets Lord Vittala here!

# SONGS OF TYAGARAJA

*(18th-19th Century A.D.)*

| | *Song* | *Rāga* |
|---|---|---|
| 1. | Jagadanandakaraka | Natai |
| 2. | Nannu palimpa | Mohanam |
| 3. | Sangeetajnanamu | Dhanyasi |
| 4. | Ramanee samaanamevaru | Kharaharapriya |
| 5. | Nidhi chala sukhamaa | Kalyani |
| 6. | Maru gelara | Jayantasree |
| 7. | Evarimaata | Kamboji |
| 8. | Soga suga | Sri Ranjani |
| 9. | Nagumomuganaleni | Abheri |
| 10. | Jnana mosaga raadaa | Poorvikalyani |

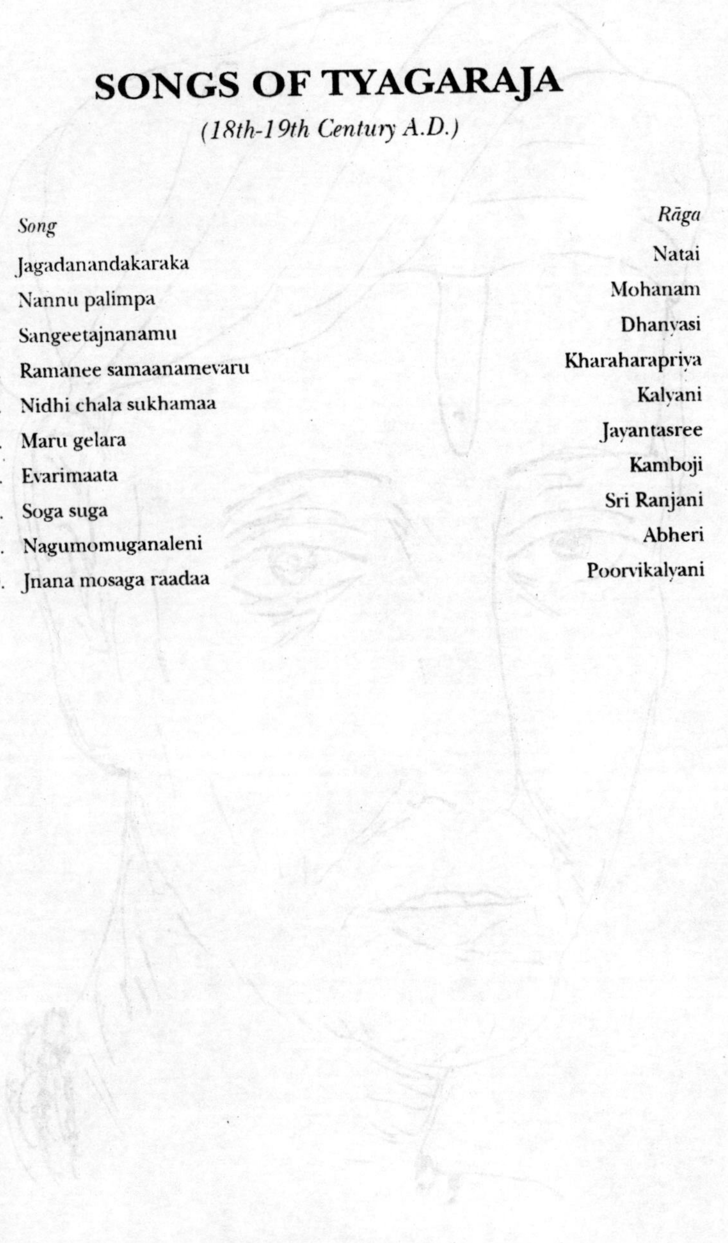

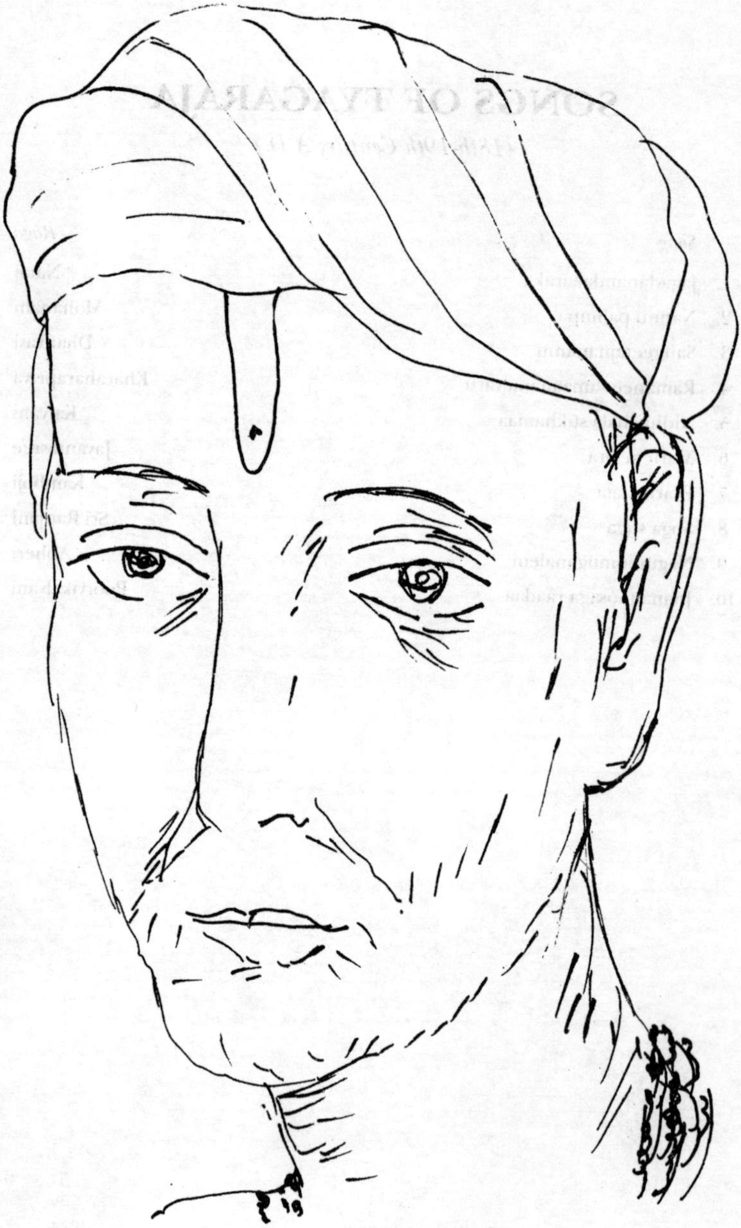

*TYAGARAJA*

# TYAGARAJA (1767-1847)

Tyagaraja, the saint composer was born in Tiruvaiyar in Tamilnadu, on 4th May 1767. He lived most of his life in Tiruvaiyar till his death on 6th January 1847.

Right from childhood he devoted himself to the worship of Lord Rama singing songs extolling his favourite deity.

He had a daughter, through whom he had a grandson, who died progeniless. Thus we do not have any descendants of saint Tyagaraja. His wife predeceased him.

Daily Tyagaraja would walk the streets of his native town singing songs and seeking alms (known as *Unchavritti*).

Tyagaraja has composed about 800 songs, most of them in his mother tongue Telugu and a few in Sanskrit.

The only travel he undertook in his life was a short pilgrimage from Tirupati to Srirangam.

Tyagaraja shied away from material possessions and refused to sing in praise of the King. He was determined to remain poor and independent.

Tyagaraja lived his own philosophy that God realisation was best achieved through *Nādopasana* (music with devotion). His songs are surfeit with an intimate devotion for Rama, though they fully reveal his deep understanding of the tenets of the Vedas and Upanishads.

The music of his compositions overpowers the lyrical content, but there is no mistaking the spiritual effect of his songs on the listener.

Purandharadasa was the grandfather of Carnatic music. Tyagaraja is one of its Trinity, the other two being Muthuswami Dikshitar and Syama Sastri.

राग : नाटै

Rāga : Nātai

.1. ''जगदा नन्द कारक'' — आदि

प. जगदानन्द कारक जय जानकी प्राणनायक (ज)

''Jagadā nanda kāraka'' — Ādi

P. Jagadānanda kāraka jaya jānakī prāṇanāyaka (Ja)

अ. गगनाधिप सत्कुलज राजराजेश्वर
सुगुणाकर सुरसेव्य भव्यदायक सदासकल (ज)

A. Gaganādhipa satkulaja rājarājeswara
Sugunā-kara surasevya bhavyadāyaka sadāsakala (Ja)

च.1. अमर दायक निचय कुमुद हित
परिपूर्णानघ सुरसुर भू-
जदधि पयोधि वासहरण
सुन्दरतर वदन सुधा मय वचो
बृन्द गोविन्द सानन्द
मावराजरास शुभ करानेक (ज)

C.1. Amara dāyaka nicaya kumuda hita
paripūrṇānagha surasura bhū-
jadadhi payodhi vāsaharaṇa
sundara tara vadana sudhā maya vaco
brunda govinda sānanda
māvarājarāpta śubh karāneka (Ja)

च.2. निगम नीरजामृतज पोषका-
निमिषवैरि वारिद समीरण
खगतुरंग सत्कविहृदायला-
गणित वानराधिप नतांघ्रियुग (ज)

C.2. nigama nīrajāmrutaja poṣakā-
nimiṣa vairi vārida samīraṇa
khagaturanga satkavihrudāya lā-
ganita vānarādhipa natānghriyuga (Ja)

1. *Jagadanandakaraka*

P. Hail! O Creator of bliss for the universe.
Hail! Beloved Lord of Sita!

A. Be victorious O! Descendant of the solar race! King of kings! Ocean of virtues! venerated by the angels, O! bestower of auspiciousness!

C.1. You are the moon among the stars of angels, you are the complete One, the stainless One! To the monkey hordes you are like the Kalpaka tree! You are the stealer of pots full of curds and milk, Your face is handsome, your words ooze nectar, You are the cowherd, full of joy, Lord of Sri, ever youthful, doing good to those who love you.

C.2. You were nourished by the nectar dripping from the lotuses of the Vedas.
Like the wind you scatter the clouds of the angels' enemies.
You ride the Garuda, you are located in the hearts of good poets,
At your feet, hordes of monkey chieftains bow down.

च.3. इन्द्र नीलमणि सन्निभापघन
चन्द्रसूर्य नयनाप्रमेय वा-
गीन्द्र जनक सकलेश शुभ्र ना-
गेन्द्र शयन शमनवैरि सन्नुत (ज)

C.3. Indra nīlamaṇi sannibhāpaghana
Candra sūrya nayanāprameya va-
gīndra janaka sakaleśa śubhra na-
gendra śayana śamana vairi sannuta (Ja)

च.4. पाद विजित मौनिशाप सवपरि-
पाल वर मन्त्र ग्रहण लोल
परमशान्त चित्त जनकजाधिप
सरोज भव वरदाखिल (ज)

C.4. Pāda vijita mauniśāpa savapari-
pāla vara mantra grahaṇa lola
parama śānta citta janakajādhipa
Saroja bhava varadākhila (Ja)

च.5. सृष्टि स्थित्यन्तकार कामित
कामित फलदा समानगात्र
शचीपतिनुताब्धि मदहरानुराग
रागराजित कथासारहित (ज)

C.5. Sruṣṭi sthityantakāra kāmita
kāmita phaladā samānagātra
śacī patinutābdhi madaharānurāga
rāgarājita kathāsārahita (Ja)

C.3. Your body is resplendent like the blue sapphire of Indra. The sun and the moon are your eyes. Your fame is unimaginable. You are the father of Brahma, the Lord of Sarasvat. You are the Lord of lords, You sleep on the silvery Adisesha, You are venerated by Siva, the Destroyer of death.

C.4. By your feet, you ended the curse of the sage (Gautama). You keep your word. You learnt the great mantras (Bala and Atibala), You are the seat of serenity, the Lord of Sita, the granter of boon to Brahma who appeared on the lotus.

C.5. You perform the three acts of creation, protection and dissolution. You fulfil myriad desires, Your beauty is peerless. You are worshipped by Indra. You destroyed the arrogance of the ocean King. You are the essence of the Ramayana story, shining with devotion and music. You give what is pleasing.

च.6. सज्जन मानसाब्धि सुधाकर कु-
सुमविमान सुरसारिपुकराब्ज
लालित चरणावगुणासुरगण
मदहरण सनातनाजनुत (ज)

C.6. Sajjana mānasābdhi sudhākara ku-
suma vimāna surasāri pukarābja
lālita caraṇāvaguṇāsuragaṇa
mada haraṇa sanātanājanuta (Ja)

च.7. ओंकार पंजरकीर पुरहर सरोजभव केशवादि-
रूप वासवरिपु जनकान्तक कला धरास घृणाकर
शरणागत जनपालन सुमनोरमण निर्विकार निगमसारतर (ज)

C.7. Omkāra panjarakīra purahara saroja bhava kesavādi-
rūpa vāsavaripu janakāntaka kalā dharāpta ghruṇākara
śaraṇāgata janapālana sumanoramaṇa nirvikāra
nigamasāratara (Ja)

च.8. कर धृत शरजालासुर मदाप हरणावनीसुर सुरावन
कवीनबिल जमौनि कृत चरित्र सन्नुत श्री त्यागराजनुत (ज)

C.8. kara dhruta śarajālāsura madāpa
haraṇāvanīsura surāvana
kavīna bila jamauni kruta caritra
sannuta śrī Tyāgarājanuta (Ja)

C.6. You are the moon rising from the sea of good men's minds. You have the Pushpaka plane. Your feet are worshipped by the lotus hands of Hanuman who defeated the demoness Suraja. You are the Destroyer of the arrogance of the wicked demons. You are eternal. You are worshipped by the four-faced Brahma.

C.7. You are the bird residing in the cage of the Pranava sound: AUM. Siva, Brahma, and Vishnu are your varied forms. You killed Ravana, the father of Indrajit. You are the beloved of the Crescentcrested Siva. You are compassionate. You protect those who seek refuge in you. You delight those with good minds. You are the changeless One. You are the essence of the Vedas.

C.8. You hold arrows in your hand. You conquer the frenzy of the demons. You are the protector of the angels and sages. You have been eulogised by the epic written by Valmiki, the Sun among poets. You are the Lord worshipped by Tyagaraja.

च.9. पुराण पुरुष नृवरात्म जा-
श्रित पराधीन खर विराध रावण
विरावणानघ पराशर मनो
हरविकृत त्यागराज सन्नुत (ज)

C.9. Purāṇa puruṣa nruvarātma ja-
śrita parādhīna khara virādha rāvaṇa
virāvaṇanagha parāśara mano-
hara vikruta tyāgarāja sannuta (Ja)

च.10. अगणित गुण कनकचेल
साल विदल नारुणाभ समान चरणा-
पार महिमाद्भुत सुकविजन
हृत्सधन सुरमुनि गणविहित
कलश नीरनिधिजारमण पापगज
नृसिंह वर त्यागराजादिनुत (ज)

C.10. Agaṇita guṇa kanakacela
sāla vidala nāruṇābha samāna caraṇā-
pāra mahimādbhuta sukavijana
hrutsadhana suramuni gaṇavihita
kalaśa nīranidhi jāramaṇa pāpagaja
nrusimha vara tyāgarājādinuta (Ja)

C.9. You are the Primordial One. You are the son of the Emperor. You are captivated by sages. You are the Destroyer of Khara, Virata and Ravana. You are sinless. You won the heart of Parasara. You are devoid of change. You are the Lord worshipped by Tyagaraja.

C.10. You have endless good qualities. You wear the yellow robe. You split apart trees. Your fame is immeasurable. You are seated in the hearts of good wondrous poets. You are the friend of angels and sages. You are the Lord of Lakshmi who rose out of the milky ocean. You are the lion destroying the elephants of sins. You are the Lord, praised by devotees like Tyagaraja.

राग : मोहनं Rāga : Mohanam

2. ''ननु पालिम्प''

प. ननु पालिम्प नडचि वच्चितिवो ? ना प्राणनाथ (न)

अ. वनजनयन नो मोमु जूचुट जी-
वनमनि नेनरुन मनसु मर्ममु तेलिसि (न)

च. सुरपति नीलमणि निभ तनुवुतो
नरमुन मुत्यपु सरुल चयमुतो
करमुन शर कोदण्ड कान्तितो (न)
धरणितनयतो; त्यागराजार्चित

"Nanu pāliṁpa"

P. Nanu pāliṁpa naḍa ci vacciti vo? Nā prāṇanātha (Na)

A. Vanajanayana no momu jūcuṭa jī-
Vanamani nenaruna manasu marmamu telisi (Na)

C. Surapati nīlamaṇi nibha tanuvuto
Naramuna mutyapu sarula cayamuto
Karamuna śara kodaṇḍa kāntito
Dharaṇitanayato; Tyāgarājārcita (Na)

2. *Nannu Palimpa*

P. To protect me, you came walking? O! Lord of my life breath!

A. O Lotus-eyed One! You came walking to protect me
knowing the secret hidden in my mind
that looking at your sweet face is the essence of my life.
(You came walking to protect me)

C. Your body resplendent like the blue sapphire of lord Indra,
wearing the cluster of pearls dancing on your chest,
holding the shining bow and arrows in your hand,
along with Sita, the daughter of the earth,
You, who are worshipped by Tyagaraja!,
came walking to protect me.

राग : धन्यासि

Rāga : Dhanyāsi

3. "संगीत ज्ञानमु"

प. संगीत ज्ञानमु भक्तिविना
सन्मार्गमु गलदे ? मनसा ! (सं)

अ. भृंगि नटेश समीरज घटज म-
तंग नारदादुलु पासिंचु (सं)

च. न्यान्यायमुलु देलुसुनु जगमुलु
मायामयमनि देलुसुनु दुर्गुण
कायजादि षड्रिपुल जयिंचु
कार्यमु देलुसुनु, त्यागराजुनिकि (सं)

"Sangīta Jñānamu"

P. Sangīta jñānamu bhaktivinā
Sanmārgamu galade? manasā! (Sa)

A. Bhrungi Naṭeśa samīraja ghaṭaja ma-
tanga Nāradādulu pāsincu (Sa)

C. Nyānyāyamulu delusunu jagamulu
Māyāmayamani delusunu durguna
kāyajādi ṣaḍripula jayincu
kāryamu delusunu, Tyāgarājuniki (Sa)

3. *Sangeetha Jnanamu*

O! Mind! Is there a righteous path superior to music and devotion?

Great Ones like Bhrungi, Nataraja, Hanuman, Agastya, Matanga and Narada adored music.

Tyagaraja knows what is right and wrong,
that the material worlds are illusory,
and also how the six evils like lust, anger, greed, illusion, arrogance and envy should be conquered.
And yet, (he feels), there is no righteous path superior to music yoked to devotion.

राग : खरहरप्रिया Rāga : Kharaharapriya

4. "राम नी समान"

प. राम नी समान मेवरु ? रघुवंशोद्धारक ! (रा)

अ. भामा मरुवम्पु मोलक भक्तियनु पंजरपु चिलुक (रा)

च. पलुकु पलुकुलकु तेने-लोलुकु माटलाडु सोद-
रुलगल हरि त्यागराज कुल विभूष ! मृदुसुभाष ! (रा)

"Rāma nī samāna"

P. Rāma nī samāna mevaru? raghuvamśoddhāraka! (Rā)

A. Bhāmā maruvampu molaka bhaktianu panjarapu ciluka (Rā)

C. Paluku palukulaku tenē-loluku māṭalādu soda-
rulagala hari tyāgarāja kula vibhūṣa! mrudusubhāṣa! (Rā)

4. *Rama Ni Samanamevaru*

O! Rama! Who can be your equal? You have uplifted the lineage of Raghu.

Your spouse Sita is like the marjoram, slender and fragrant in form.

She is the bird residing in the cage of your devotion.

Your brothers speak honeyed words. You are the Jewel of Tyagaraja's family.

You are soft spoken.

O! Rama! Who can be your equal?

राग : कल्याणी Rāga : Kalyāni

5. "निधि चाल सुखमा"

प. निधि चाल सुखमा ? रामुनि
सन्निधि सेव सुखमा ? निजमुग बल्कु मनसा ! (नि)

अ. दधि नवनीत क्षीरमुलु रुचियो ? दाश-
रथि ध्यान भजन सुधा रसमु रुचियो ? (नि)

च. दम शममनु गङ्गास्नानमु सुखमा ?
कर्दम दुर्विषय कूप स्नानमु सुखमा ?
ममत बन्धन युत नरस्तुति सुखमा ?
सुमति त्यागराजनुतुनि कीर्तन सुखमा ? (नि)

P. Nidhi cāla sukhamā? Rāmuni
sannidhi seva sukhamā? Nijamuga balku manasā! (Ni)

A. Dadhi navanīta kṣīramulu ruciyo? Dāśa-
rathi dhyāna bhajana sudhā rasamu ruciyo? (Ni)

C. Dama śamamanu Gaṅgāsnānamu sukhamā?
Kardama durviṣaya kūpa snānamu sukhamā?
Mamata bandhana yuta narastuti sukhamā?
Sumati Tyāgarājanutuni kīrtana sukhamā? (Ni)

5. *Nidhi Chala Sukhama*

P. Does wealth give greater happiness or worship in Rama's sanctum?
O! Mind! Tell me the truth.

A. Are curds, butter, milk etc. tasty?
Or meditating on the son of Dasaratha?
(O! Mind! Tell me the truth.)

C. Does bathing in the Ganga with discipline and serenity give joy?
Or bathing in the dirty well of transient pleasures?
(O! Mind! Tell me the truth.)
Is praising arrogant mortal men joyous?
Or singing the praises of the goodminded Lord, worshipped by Tyagaraja?
(O! Mind! Tell me the truth.)

राग : जयन्तश्री Rāga : Jayantaśrī

6. मरुगेलरा

प. मरुगेलरा ? ओ राघव ! (म)

अ. मरुगेल ? चराचररूप ! परा-
त्परा ! सूर्यसुधाकरलोचन ! (म)

च. अन्नि नीवनुचु नन्तरङ्गमुन
दिन्नगा वेदकि तेलिसिकोटिनय्य
निन्नेगानि मदि नेन्नजाल नोरुल
नन्नुब्रोववय्य, त्यागराजनुत (म)

Marugelarā

P. Marugelarā? O Rāghava! (Ma)

A. Marugela? Carācararūpa! Parā-
tparā! Sūryasudhākara locana! (Ma)

C. Anni nīvanucu nantarangamuna
Dinnagā vedaki telisikoṭinayya
Ninnegāni madi nennayjāla norula
Nannubrovavayya, Tyāgarājanuta (Ma)

6. *Marugelara*

O! Rama, Descendant of Raghu! Why are you hiding your self?
You have manifested yourself as all the animate and inanimate beings of the universe,
You are the Supreme of the Supreme,
Your eyes are the Sun and the moon,
Hence why hide yourself?

I have realised, after deep heartsearching, that you are the whole cosmos.
I cannot think of anyone else but you.
Please protect me, O! Lord, worshipped by Tyagaraja!

राग : काम्भोजि

Rāga : Kāmbhoji

7. "एवरिमाट विन्नावो"

प. एवरिमाट विन्नावो, रावो-यिन्दु लेवो! भलि! भलि! (ए)

अ. अवनिलो नार्षेय पौरुषेय
मन्दि चोद्य मेरुग लेनय्य (ए)

च. भक्त पराधीनु डनुचु-परम भागवतुल
व्यक्त रूपुडै पलिकिन मुच्चट-युक्तमनुचु नुंटि
शक्ति गल महादेवुडु नीवनि संतोषमुन नुंटि;
सत्त चित्तुडगु त्यागराजनुत!
सत्य सन्धुडनुकोंटि निललो (ए)

"Evarimāṭa vinnāvo"

P. Evarimāṭa vinnāvo, rāvō-yindu levo! bhali! bhali! (Ev)

A. Avanilo nārṣeya pauruṣeya
mandi codya meruga lenayya (Ev)

C. bhakta parādhīnudanucu-parama bhāgavatula
vyakta rūpudai palikina muccaṭay-uktamanucu nunti
śakti gala mahādevudu nīvani santoṣamuna nunti;
satta cittuḍagu tyāgarājanuta!
satya sandhuḍanu konti nilalo (Ev)

7. *Evari Mata*

By whose words have you been carried away?
Why have you not come and be here?
Well, Well!

Even after delving deep into the revelations of sages and sacred scriptures,
I am unable to decipher this riddle.

I had believed that you are subservient to your devotees,
on the basis of what you had told your supreme devotees in your various incarnations.
I had rejoiced that You are the Omnipotent Being!
O! Lord, worshipped by Tyagaraja! I thought you were firm minded and truthful, (What has happened?)
By whose words have you been carried away?

राग : श्रीरंजनि

Rāga : Sreeranjani

8. "सोगसुगा मृदंग"

प. सोगसुगा मृंदगतालमु जतगूर्च निनु
सोक्कजेयु धीरुडेव्वडो (सो)

अ. निगमशिरोर्थमु गल्गिन
निजवाक्कुलतो, स्वरशुद्धमुतो (सो)

च. यति विश्रम सद्भक्ति विरति
द्राक्षारस नवरसयुत
कृतिचे भजियिंचु युक्ति
त्यागराजुनि तरमा ? श्रीराम ! (सो)

"Sogasugā mrudanga"

P. Sogasugā mrudangatālamu jatagūrca ninu
sokkajeyu dhīrudevvado (So)

A. Nigamaśirorthamu galgina
nijavākkulato, swaraśuddhamuto (So)

C. Yati viśrama sadbhakti virati
drākṣārasa navarasayuta
krutice bhajiyincu yukti
Tyāgarājuni taramā? Śrīrāma! (So)

8. *Sogasuga Mridanga Talamu*

Who is that brave man who can hold you in a spell by singing songs which are a blend of meaningful words, purity of melody and soulful rhythm?

O! Sri Rama! is it possible for this Tyagaraja

to sing songs in your praise combining cadence, feeling, supreme devotion, purity of melody, the sweetness of grapes and the nine emotions?

राग : आभेरि

Rāga : Ābheri

9. ''नगुमोमु गनलेनि''

प. नगुमोमु गनलेनि नाजालि तेलिसि
नन्नुब्रोवरा राद श्री रघुवर नी (न)

अ. नागराजधर! नीदुपरिवारु लेल्ल
ओगिबोधन जेसेवारुलु गारे? यिटुलुण्डुदुरे? नी (न)

च. खगराजु नी यानति विनि वेग चन लेडो?
गगनानि किलकू बहु दूरं बनिनाडो? -
जगमेले परमात्मा! येवरितो मोरलिडुदु?
वग चूपकु तालनु नन्नेलुकोरा त्यागराजनुत! (न)

"Nagumomu ganaleni"

P. Nagumomu ganaleni nājāli telisi
nannubrovarā rāda Śrīraghuvara nī (Na)

A. Nāgarājadhara! nīduparivāru lella
Ogibodhana jesevārulu gāre? yiṭuluṇḍudure? nī (Na)

C. Khagarājunī yānati vini vega cana ledo?
Gaganāni kilakū bahu dūraṁ baninādo? -
Jagamele paramātmā! yevarito moraliḍudu?
Vaga cūpaku tālanu nannelukorā Tyāgarājanuta! (Na)

9. *Nagu Momu Gana Leni*

O! Greatest of the Raghu race!
Can't you come and confer your grace on me,
knowing fully well my sorrow in not being able to see your sweet, smiling face?

O! Lord who held the (Govardhana) mountain with your hand!
Aren't your attendants giving you the right advice?
Didn't Garuda, the King of birds come flying fast at your command?
Or did he tarry on the pretext that the earth is too far away from heaven?

O! Supreme Soul who guard the universe!
To whom else can I plead?

Don't be averse to me. I cannot bear it.
Accept me, You who are worshipped by Tyagaraja.

राग : पूर्विकल्याणि

Rāga : Poorvikalyāṇi

10. ''ज्ञान मोसग रादा''

प. ज्ञान मोसग रादा! गरुडगमन! वादा! (ज्ञा)

अ. नी नाममुचे नामदि निर्मलमैनदि (ज्ञा)

च. परमात्मुडु जीवात्मुडु पदुनालुगु लोकमुलु
सुरकिन्नर किम्पुरुषुलु नारदादि मुनुलु
परिपूर्ण! निष्कलङ्क! निरवधिसुखदायक!
वर त्यागराजार्चित! वारमु तानने (ज्ञा)

"Jñāna mosaga rādā"

P. Jñāna mosaga rādā! Garuḍagamana! vādā (Jñā)

A. Nī nāmamuce nāmadi nirmalamainadi (Jñā)

C. Paramātmuḍu jīvātmudu padunālugu lokamulu
Surakinnara kiṁpuruṣulu nāradādi munulu
Paripūrṇa! niṣkalaṅka! niravadhisukhadāyaka
Vara Tyāgarājārcita! vāramu tānane (Jñā)

10. *Jnana Mosaga Rada*

Can't you give me knowledge? O! rider of Garuda (the King of birds)!
Is there any contention between us?

My mind has been purified by the recitation of your name.

Can't you confer on me the realisation that I am the individual soul as well as the Supreme Self, that I am the fourteen worlds, and celestial beings like Kinnaras, Kimpurushas, and saints like Narada.

O! Complete One! O! Stainless One! Bestower of endless bliss!

O! Venerable One, worshipped by Tyagaraja! why contend with me?